THINK About
Guns in America

The THINK Series Editors: William N. Thorndike, Jr.
                              Ramsey R. Walker

Executive Editor: Doug Hardy
Researcher: Martha T. Griffith

Text Designer: Joyce C. Weston
Jacket Designer: Georg Brewer
Copyeditor: Victoria Haire
Photo Researcher: Diane Hamilton
Text Illustrator: Peter Zale
Research Assistant: Caitlin Dixon

The THINK Series

THINK About
Guns in America

Helen Strahinich

Walker and Company
New York

First published in the United States of America in 1992
by Walker Publishing Company, Inc.

Published simultaneously in Canada by Thomas Allen & Son
Canada, Limited, Markham, Ontario

Library of Congress Cataloging-in-Publication Data
Strahinich, Helen.
    Think about guns in America / Helen Strahinich.
        p.   cm. —(The Think series)
    Includes bibliographical references and index.
    Summary: Discusses in an evenhanded manner the
ownership and use of guns in America, the relationship of
guns to violence, the role of the National Rifle Association,
gun control laws, etc.
    ISBN 0-8027-8104-7. —ISBN 0-8027-7356-7 (pbk.)
    1. Gun control—United States—Juvenile
literature.   2. Firearms—United States—Juvenile
literature.   [1. Gun control.   2. Firearms.]
I. Title.   II. Series.
HV7436.S77   1992
363.3'3'0973—dc20   91-10616
                                                              CIP
                                                               AC

Photographs of guns in Chapter 1 courtesy of the National
Rifle Association; "Compendium of State Laws Governing
Handguns, 1990," in the Appendix, courtesy of the National
Rifle Association.

Printed in the United States of America
10   9   8   7   6   5   4   3   2   1

CONTENTS

THINK About
Guns in America

INTRODUCTION

Picture this debate in your town hall. The subject of the debate is guns. Tension grows as the first speaker comes to the podium. He says your town has too many guns. He's scared about violence on your streets. He's afraid for his family. He wants new gun-control laws—to keep guns out of the hands of criminals and crazies. There are cheers and boos when the first speaker leaves the podium.

The second speaker tells the audience that there's no such thing as a bad gun. Only bad people using guns. He says that law-abiding Americans need guns for protection. He reminds the audience of their constitutional right to own guns. He says he's afraid of violence, too; but controlling guns is not the way to control violence. Tougher criminal laws and stricter sentences are the answer. As the second speaker leaves the podium, there are more cheers and more boos.

The debate continues. Other speakers give statistics and offer proposals. They tell personal stories about how guns have hurt them—or helped them. The audience is divided up the middle, each side certain that their position is right. Everybody seems angry and scared. And there appears to be no room for compromise. Or is there?

GUNS "Я" US

Whether you love guns or hate them, one thing is certain: guns are as American as hamburgers and hotdogs. They've been part of American life for hundreds of years. American settlers and pioneers relied on smoothbore muskets to protect their homes and to hunt for food. During the Revolutionary War, colonists won independence from the British with their flintlock rifles. During the Civil War, Northerners and Southerners battled over slavery and states' rights with their Colt .44s, their Spencer Carbines, and their rifled muskets. And during the twentieth century, Americans hauled automatic rifles and machine guns to Europe and Asia to fight two world wars and, later, two more wars in Korea and Vietnam.

Today, Americans own more guns than the citizens of any other Western country—200 million guns by recent estimates. That's almost one gun for every man, woman, and child in the United States. And some Americans are asking whether the cost of guns—in violence and fear—is too high. But other Americans insist that guns are as necessary now as they were in the past—for protecting their homes and their freedom.

So what should be done about guns in America? It's one of the hottest questions around, one that affects teenagers and young adults more than any other group. If you don't have an answer, now's the time to start thinking about it.

GUN OWNERSHIP

In the three minutes or so that it takes you to read this page, American gun manufacturers will produce about twenty new guns. That's one gun every nine seconds or four million guns every year. Americans keep guns for hunting, for target practice, for sport shooting, for work, for collecting, and for protection.

A wide variety of weapons is available to the millions of American gun buyers. (*Copyright* Washington Post; *reprinted by permission of the D.C. Public Library*)

Over the past twenty years, gun ownership in the United States has been on the rise—along with the population. America is the largest nation of gun-hunters in the world, with an estimated twenty million hunters and 13,521 gun clubs nationwide. One in every seventy Americans belongs to the National Rifle Association (NRA), an organization that promotes markmanship and gun safety and also lobbies against gun control. Its membership, which grew almost 300 percent over the past decade, is now 2.8 million. Presidents John F. Kennedy, Theodore Roosevelt, Dwight Eisenhower, Richard Nixon, Ronald Reagan, and George Bush have all been card-carrying members of the NRA.

THE TOLL

In the ten hours or so that it takes you to read this book, about thirty-four American civilians will die from gunfire. That's eighty-two Americans on the average each day, 30,000 every year. In the United States, guns account for three out of five murders in this country; handguns for 47 percent of all murders.

The toll of gun violence on teenagers and young adults is especially high. The number of Americans under the age of thirty-five who were killed with guns has doubled in the past twenty years. In 1989, over half (52 percent) of all victims murdered with firearms were twenty to thirty-four years old. Slightly over 66 percent were between the ages of fifteen and thirty-four.

Why are teenagers and young adults so often victims of gun violence? According to the experts, many factors may cause a young person to resort to violence—and to pick up a gun if it is available. Some say that unemployment, the use of drugs and alcohol, personal problems, or lack of maturity lead to such violence. Others blame permissive gun laws that have made it easy for young people to acquire guns and to use them for violent purposes.

THE DEBATE OVER GUN CONTROL

Most Americans want an end to gun violence. But they disagree on two basic questions: Why do we have gun violence? And what should we do to stop it? Those who favor gun control and those who don't have battled for years over these questions.

In general, pro- gun controllers favor laws that make guns—or certain kinds of guns—harder to get. They believe that too many guns lead to gun violence. Anti-gun controllers, on the other hand, want fewer laws and fewer restrictions on guns. They believe that criminals will get guns and use them whether or not legislators pass gun-control laws.They favor stiff sentences to keep felons off the street.

On each side of the gun question, there are hardliners who allow little room for compromise. Some gun-control advocates, for example, want to ban all guns. And some anti- gun controllers view any restrictions on guns as a threat to their freedom. But most Americans favor a more moderate position, according to recent surveys. These opinion polls show—as others have over the years—that the majority of Americans support the right of civilians to buy and own firearms. Recent surveys also show that 70 percent of Americans, including members of the NRA, favor registration of handguns.

STATISTICS: WHAT DO THEY MEAN?

As you read this book, you will be exposed to historical accounts, statistics, and surveys. Keep in mind that different people, depending on their points of view, may disagree on how to interpret the same information. Or they may present different accounts of the same events. Or they may use only those facts that support their personal opinions. To determine the number of guns manufactured in a given year, for instance, one group might use manufacturers' reports while another might use reports from the Bureau of Alcohol, Tobacco, and Firearms. Each could say they were using objective facts. Likewise, two surveys might report different findings on the same subject. For example, two polls of gunowners' attitudes toward gun control could show conflicting results. The way the pollsters phrase their questions can affect the results.

This is not meant to suggest that all information is equally valid. The point is to read critically. Consider

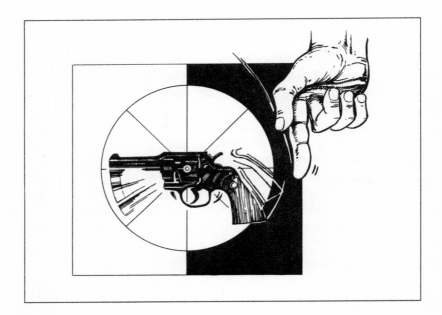

different interpretations. Look at the source of each statistic or survey. And question the point of view of each source.

WHERE DO YOU STAND?

Where do you stand on the gun questions? Maybe you believe that gun ownership *without restrictions* is the right of all Americans. Maybe you believe guns are instruments of evil that should be banned from every community. Maybe you support a position that is somewhere between these two extremes. Or maybe you haven't figured out yet where you stand.

Because the gun debate is both complicated and personal, this book will discuss both sides. It will review many facts and statistics on the subject of firearms. It will explore some controversial issues such as guns and crime, gun accidents, and gun suicides; and other issues such as firearm safety; kinds of guns; the history of firearms; and gun laws. You'll have to decide how you believe gun violence can be stopped. You'll have to decide how you would react to the news that your friend was buying a firearm. You'll have to decide what guns mean to you.

REVIEW QUESTIONS

1. How many new guns do American gun manufacturers produce in one hour? One day? One week?
2. How many Americans die from gunfire every week? Every month?
3. What age group is most victimized by gun violence? Why do you think this is so?
4. What are the basic views of the advocates of gun control?
5. What are the basic views of those against gun control?
6. Would you be surprised to find out that your next-door neighbor owned a gun? Why or why not?

1 | Kinds of Guns

Maybe you've heard about handguns, "Saturday night specials," semiautomatic assault rifles, sawed-off shotguns, or plastic pistols. The gun-control debate often focuses on one kind of gun. But how are these guns the same? How are they different?

In this book, the term *gun* means any firearm. However, this chapter does not deal with illegal or highly destructive weapons, such as machine guns and explosives. These weapons do not account for a significant part of the gun violence on American streets or in American homes. They are not an important part of the gun-control debate.

CLASSES OF GUNS

There are three basic types of guns: *handguns, rifles,* and *shotguns.* You've probably seen all three kinds of guns at the movies or on television. Cowboys and sheriffs carry rifles and shotguns—also known as *long guns*—in Western movies. Policemen and detectives tote handguns in cop-and-robber flicks.

A rifle, or long gun, has a *stock*—or handle—that fits to the shoulder and a long *barrel*—or tube—through which a bullet is released. The rifle barrel is thick and heavy with a small opening at the end. All long guns have grooves in their barrels, called *rifling*, which make bullets spin, causing them to fly in straight lines.

A shotgun looks a lot like a rifle—with a long barrel and stock. But the shotgun barrel is thin-walled. It has a larger opening than a rifle barrel.

Handguns have a short barrel. They are small enough to hold in your hand—hence, the name. Handgun barrels, like rifle barrels, have rifling inside the tube.

GUN PARTS

All three classes of guns have many of the same parts. The pictures on this page show the parts of a common handgun.

All guns have these parts: (1) a *chamber*, the part that holds the cartridge at the instant of firing; (2) a *stock*, or *grip*, the part that is held during firing; (3) a *barrel*, the tube through which a bullet is discharged;

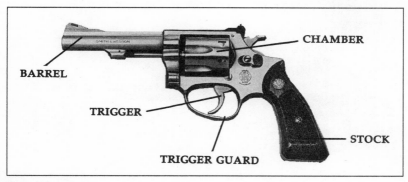

Parts of a gun.

(4) a *muzzle*, the end of the gun through which a bullet is shot; (5) a *trigger*, the part of the lock mechanism that, when pulled, releases the gear and/or firing pin; and (6) a *trigger guard*, the part that keeps the trigger from accidentally releasing.

Guns are identified according to their class—rifles, shotguns, and handguns. They are also identified according to their *action*—the way they are loaded, fired, and unloaded.

TYPES OF RIFLES AND SHOTGUNS

Rifles may have *bolt* or *lever action*. Shotguns may have pump action. Both can be found with semiautomatic action. Some shotguns also have break action, usually found on single or double barrel shotguns.

Bolt-action rifles work like the bolt of a door. Bolt action is the most common type of rifle action.

Lever-action rifles have levers under the stock. They work like the lever of an automobile tire iron. These guns were commonly used in the Old West.

Pump-action shotguns work by pumping the handle under the barrel backward and forward. Pump action is the most common type of shotgun action.

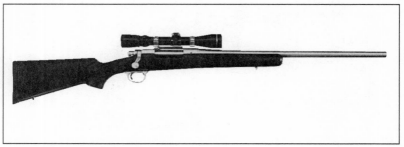

Bolt-action rifle.

Lever-action rifle.

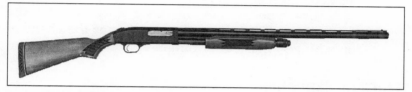

Pump-action shotgun.

Hunting was a significant livelihood for Americans as recently as the 1930s. *(Courtesy of The Library of Congress)*

Rifles and shotguns that use a semiautomatic action fire one bullet for each pull of the trigger. The force of the firing bullet ejects the spent cartridge and inserts a new one into the chamber. Semiautomatic firearms hold their ammunition in magazines. Some rifles have detachable magazines. Semiautomatics are also common long guns.

A fifth type of shotgun has a break action. The *break-action shotgun* opens and closes at the chamber on a hinge—like a door hinge.

TYPES OF HANDGUNS

There are two types of handguns: *revolvers* and *semiautomatics*.

A revolver has a *cylinder* that rotates each time the gun is fired. The cylinder has five to nine *chambers* where the ammunition can be stored.

Semiautomatic rifle.

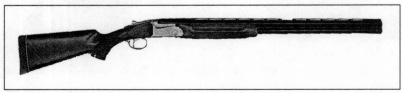

Break-action shotgun.

Semiautomatic handguns or pistols—like some semiautomatic long guns—usually have removable magazines that hold the ammunition.

COMMON CRIMINAL GUNS

Sawed-off shotgun. This is an old shotgun. It has a break action with a double barrel and double trigger. Although often used for bird and small game hunting, the ends of the barrels have been sawed off. Criminals often illegally saw off the barrels of shotguns or rifles so they can hide them under a car seat or inside a coat.

Glock 17 pistol. This is a police handgun. It is semiautomatic. The magazine is in the grip. It holds seventeen rounds of ammunition. The frame is made of high-tech plastic, but the internal working parts are made of metal. Many gun-control advocates label

Sawed-off shotgun.

Glock 17 pistol.

this type of gun a "plastic" gun and call for them to be banned on the claim that they are harder to detect than all-metal guns. These guns are very widely used by law enforcement officers.

Smith & Wesson .38-caliber revolver. This is another widely used law enforcement sidearm. The cylinder holds six cartridges. It is also known as a *six-shooter*.

Raven .25-caliber. This semiautomatic handgun is under five inches long. It is small enough to hide in clothing or shoes. It costs about $70. It is a popular personal protection gun.

.22-caliber revolver. This revolver is often referred to by gun-control advocates as a *Saturday Night Special*. It is light, cheap, flimsy—and easy to come by. These guns are one of the most widely owned firearms in America.

Colt Commando .38 Snubnose. You've probably seen this kind of gun in old detective movies. It is some-

Smith & Wesson .38-caliber revolver.

Raven .25-caliber revolver.

.22-caliber revolver.

.38 Snubnose.

times nicknamed a *snubby* or *belly gun* (because it can be carried under the belt). Some off-duty police carry snubbies.

REVIEW QUESTIONS

1. How are guns identified?
2. What are the basic types of rifles? Types of shotguns? Types of handguns?
3. How are handguns and rifles the same? How are they different?
4. Why do you think some groups want to outlaw handguns but not rifles and shotguns?
5. Why do you think sawed-off shotguns are illegal?
6. Why do you think it is against the law to import "Saturday night specials"?

2 The Wild and Woolly History of Guns

You have to go back almost five hundred years to the days of the first explorers and settlers to find the earliest guns in America. In the untamed new land, guns were a necessity. Every household needed firearms for hunting and protection. They became a way of life. The story of America's guns follows the path of America's general history: the wars and the army, the march westward, the spirit of invention, the market economy, the patriots and the outlaws, the presidents and the average citizens.

EUROPEAN SETTLERS AND THEIR FIREARMS

The first American settlers carried smoothbore muskets—heavy shoulder guns without any rifling—from the Old World to their New World homes. These early colonial guns were neither very efficient nor very accurate. The firing mechanisms were unrefined. Each shot took minutes to load. And the shooter was lucky to hit a still deer at sixty yards.

Not all colonial guns were smoothbore muskets. German and Swiss immigrants, whose compatriots had been using rifles since the early 1600s, came to Pennsylvania in the early 1700s. They brought along their *jaegers*. Jaegers (which means *hunters* in German) were hunting guns with large bores and broad butts. Accurate at 100 yards, the jaeger rifles were also much faster to load than their predecessors.

The first distinctly American gun—the *Kentucky Flintlock rifle*, also known as the *American rifle*—developed from the jaeger. Backwoods gunsmiths modified the German firearm for frontier life. The slender, graceful, Kentucky rifle was longer, lighter, and easier to handle than the jaeger. Its smaller bore saved both gunpowder and lead. Its stock, decorated in silver, came from local woods—maple, cherry, or walnut. Woodsmen like Daniel Boone used it for hunting and protection. By the mid-1700s, the Kentucky rifle was in general use among the colonists.

Weapons are inseparable from even the most romantic images of American frontier settlers such as Daniel Boone. (Courtesy of The Library of Congress)

GUNS AND THE AMERICAN REVOLUTION

The accuracy of the Kentucky rifles served the colonial army well during the American Revolution. Ace marksmen terrorized the British camp with their Kentucky rifles by sniping at officers from unheard-of distances. For the big engagements, however, Kentucky rifles didn't load or fire as fast as newer smoothbore muskets. Most Revolutionary War battles were fought standing up, with masses of soldiers in formation exchanging volleys. Individual targets weren't the point. A soldier in the battlefield needed speed to knock over as many enemy bodies as he could. In the battlefield, the new, quick-loading smoothbore muskets—which allowed a trained soldier to fire four shots per minute—were crucial weapons.

THE NEXT 100 YEARS

During the 100 years following the American Revolution, numerous events, as well as the need for protection on the frontier, increased the demand for guns and brought about a gun-making revolution. These events included:

- The War of 1812 against England
- The westward expansion of the colonies
- The Indian campaigns
- The war with Mexico (1846–48)
- The Civil War (1861–65)

The Hall Rifle

In 1811, John Hall from Portland, Maine, patented a rifle that loaded through a chamber at the back of the barrel—not through the muzzle, or front, of the barrel. Hall's timing appeared perfect for a debut of his gun in the War of 1812. But he was unable to interest the U.S. Army in adopting his rifle until 1819—five years after the war ended.

John Hall himself set up the assembly line that produced the *Hall rifles*—the first firearms with fully interchangeable parts. Hall wasn't the first person to try mass-producing firearms with interchangeable parts, but his was the first big success. (Eli Whitney, inventor of the cotton gin, had tried with limited success to mass-produce a firearm twenty years earlier.) The Hall rifles were in service for over twenty-five years: in small Indian campaigns, in the war with Mexico, and even at the beginning of the Civil War.

Colt Revolvers

Samuel Colt used the assembly-line principle in 1836 to mass-produce revolvers for the first time. But he closed his Paterson, New Jersey factory when no large government contracts materialized for his *Colt Patent revolver*. During the war with Mexico, government contracts were more lucrative. In 1848, Colt opened a factory in Hartford, Connecticut, where he produced many revolver models.

The Colt *Peacemaker* was one of his most famous guns. Production on this six-shooter began in 1873. A standard army pistol, it was used in all the important Indian campaigns after 1873. The Peacemaker was the preferred revolver among cowboys, frontiersmen, miners, sheriffs, and outlaws. Like other Colts, it was also known as a *plowhandle, thumbuster, six-gun,* and *equalizer.*

Derringers

Around 1848, Philadelphia gunsmith John Deringer gave his name to a type of short-barreled pocket pistol—the *Deringer*. A powerful little firearm, it had a curled butt, a rifled barrel, and a black stock with silver mountings. It was easily concealable, accurate

to six or seven feet, and deadly. On April 14, 1865, John Wilkes Booth used this type of gun to assassinate President Abraham Lincoln.

Along with the bowie knife, the Deringer pistol was one of the most popular frontier weapons before the Civil War. So popular, in fact, that many manufacturers copied Deringer's model and disguised their theft by changing the name slightly—to *derringer*—in order to avoid a conviction for trademark infringement.

Civil War Guns

The most common Civil War gun, among Northerners and Southerners, was the *rifled musket*. With a new kind of bullet, the *Minié ball,* these firearms combined speed and accuracy. They were muzzle-loaders that fired two times a minute in combat. During the bloody Civil War that took over 700,000 lives, more men were killed by a rifled musket than any other weapon. Within ten years, however, the rifled musket was outdated—replaced by a new kind of arm, the *breechloader.* These guns, like the Hall rifle, loaded not through the muzzle but from the breech behind the barrel.

A number of breechloaders and repeating firearms were used experimentally, or on a limited basis, during the Civil War. Christopher M. Spencer from Manchester, Connecticut, designed the *Spencer rifle,* the first successful magazine repeater. It shot seven times as fast as the standard musket—fourteen to fifteen shots per minute.

But few of these firearms saw action before the spring of 1863—because the Union Army's conservative chief of ordnance, Brigadier General James W. Ripley, didn't trust breechloaders. Some Spencers were purchased privately, however, and the demand for these guns grew among the soldiers. Eventually, the government purchased over 100,000 Spencer rifles and Spencer carbines. A carbine is a short, lightweight rifle.

Likewise, Oliver Winchester, a New Haven, Connecticut, gun manufacturer, tried to sell the *Henry rifle*—designed by his plant manager, B. Tyler Henry—to the Union Army. Abraham Lincoln received a copy of this light but powerful, magazine-fed firearm, capable of shooting 120 rounds in under six minutes. But like Spencer, Winchester had no luck with the chief of ordnance. However, soldiers and officers as well as cowboys, prospectors, lawmen, and bandits bought over 10,000 Henry rifles in a three-year period. By the end of the Civil War, Winchester's company was prospering. The Henry rifle was the predecessor of the *Winchester repeater,* sometimes described as "the rifle that won the West."

Dr. Richard Gatling invented a quick-firing gun during the Civil War. This ten-barreled, hand-cranked weapon, a forerunner of the modern machine gun, was capable of firing 800 shots per minute. In typical fashion, the Union Army did not embrace this new weapon, although the Confederate Army used their own quick-firing guns. Gatling gave civilian demonstrations, hoping to promote his weapon. In 1865, some Union commanders ordered Gatling's quick-firing guns. But none of them were delivered before the war ended. Later, Colt manufactured the *Gatling*—also known as the *Gat.* It saw action in the Spanish-American War.

GUNS AND INDIANS

After the Civil War, the U.S. Army decided to adopt breechloading rifles and carbines. A decision was made to convert them into breechloaders at the Springfield Arsenal in Massachusetts. The result was the *Springfield rifle* and *Springfield carbine.* The Springfields were simple to operate, hard-hitting, and effective at long ranges. They were used in Indian campaigns, the Spanish-American War, and World War I.

In most engagements, Indians were not well armed. Fewer than half of their warriors owned guns. And Indian firepower rarely matched that of the Army. Most Indian firearms were flintlocks, light (for carrying on horseback), and easy to handle. Acquired by trade for furs, these Indian firearms went by many names: *Northwest gun, Hudson's Bay fuke, Indian gun, Mackinaw gun, Indian musket,* and *trade gun.*

THE WILD WEST

Many stories of glamour and mystery have been told about gunfighters of the Old West. But how much is fact? How much is legend? What were they really like?

James Butler ("Wild Bill") Hickok was a gambler and buffalo hunter, who became a marshal of Abilene, Texas, in 1871. Some historians, however, believe Marshal Hickok worked harder to protect saloonkeepers than Abilene's average citizens. He once brawled with the U.S. Seventh Cavalry and killed three soldiers. Afterward, he had to flee because the cavalry wanted him—dead or alive. In 1876, at age thirty-nine, Hickok was shot and killed with a Colt during a card game in a Deadwood City saloon.

Over twenty movies have glamorized the life of William H. ("Billy the Kid") Bonney—with actors like Paul Newman and Gary Cooper playing the outlaw. But historians have described the *real* William Bonney as a pathological killer, who shot most of his twenty-one victims in the back. In 1881, Sheriff Pat Garrett gunned down "the Kid" because he had murdered a Lincoln County, New Mexico sheriff and his deputies. William Bonney was twenty-two years old.

Movies also turned Jesse James into a hero, even though he was the leader of a gang that held up eleven banks, seven trains, and three stagecoaches over a fifteen-year period. He also killed sixteen peo-

Western reality was far from romantic: in fifteen years, Jesse James used his guns to kill sixteen times. (Courtesy of The Library of Congress)

ple. Eventually, a member of Jesse's own gang killed him for reward money.

As for Sheriff Wyatt Earp, modern historians say that movies about this part-time lawman only tell part of the truth. Like Wild Bill, Sheriff Earp was a gambler and barroom bouncer, who was probably on the wrong side of the law at times. According to one rumor of the day, the 1881 gun fight at O.K. Corral in Tombstone, Arizona—where Earp, Doc Holliday, and Earp's brothers Virgil and Morgan wiped out the McLowry gang—was nothing more than a cover-up of the sheriff's part in a stagecoach holdup.

The idealized legends of the Old West didn't begin in Hollywood. The perpetrators were nineteenth-century businessmen—hack newsmen, Western show promotors, and publishers of dime novels. According to one account, scout Kit Carson was once asked about the cover of a dime novel that showed him killing seven Indians and rescuing a maiden in distress. He is said to have commented, "I ain't got no recollection of it."

The glamorizing of the Old West may have started in 1869 when William ("Buffalo Bill") Cody—former pony-express rider, buffalo hunter, Indian fighter, and scout—met journalist Edward C. Judson, who used the byline Ned Buntline. After their meeting,

Judson began writing a serial about Cody's adventures called *Buffalo Bill, King of the Border Men*. Meanwhile, Cody produced Western melodramas that toured the United States. Later, he organized the famous Wild West shows, featuring gun shooting, rope tricks, and fancy riding with stars like Buffalo Bill himself and Annie Oakley. Wild West extravaganzas, cheap novels, and fanciful news reports by the likes of Judson fueled the imaginations of East Coast Americans.

The cowboys themselves—most of them peace-loving, law-abiding citizens—also helped build the swashbuckling legend. In real life, they steered clear of gunfights. For the benefit of visiting Easterners, however, they staged phony shootouts and lynchings at the train stations. After a train pulled in, someone would fire a shot. Then a cowboy would lug in a friend who was pretending to be a dead corpse. There might also be a fake lynching—with a dummy, of course—while, on board the train, women and children screamed.

GUNS IN WORLD WAR I

During the twenty-five year period before World War I, weapons and gunpower became deadlier. Automatic firearms came into their own: first, *Borchart's pistol*, a forerunner of the *Lugar*, manufactured in Germany in 1903; followed by *Colt's automatic pistol*, adopted by the U.S. Army in 1905; and then the *Browning automatic rifle*, introduced in 1917, when the United States entered World War I.

Machine guns caused half of the seven million casualties in that gory war. Hiram Maxim, from

Maine, invented the first automatic machine gun in 1885. Before Maxim's invention, all machine guns had been hand-cranked. The explosion of cartridges powered Maxim's gun until all the ammunition was used. John Browning developed another famous machine gun—the *Colt-Browning*—a few years later. This belt-fed automatic was capable of firing 400 rounds per minute at 2,000 yards. John Thompson's submachine gun (1921) never saw action in World War I. Under ten pounds, the lightweight *tommy gun* had the firepower of a machine gun. But an armistice was signed before Thompson could sell his guns.

THE GANGSTER ERA

After World War I, the military market for the tommy gun dried up. But many of these guns found their way into criminal hands. They were small, easy to conceal, and powerful. The first gang use of a Thompson submachine gun was in Chicago during the Beer Wars of 1925, when mobsters were fighting for a share of the lucrative trade in illegal liquor. A few years later, tommys made their way to the New York underworld. Soon after, New York City was dubbed the crime capital of America.

Dozens of gangster movies—such as *Public Enemy*, starring James Cagney; *King of the Underworld*, with Humphrey Bogart; and *Little Caesar*, starring Edward G. Robinson—glamorized the lives of underworld toughs and professional criminals. Like Old-West outlaws before them, these mobsters captured the fancy of many Americans. Al Capone, John Dillinger, Bugs Moran, George ("Machine Gun") Kelly, and Pretty Boy Floyd became household names. So,

too, did the G-men and other FBI agents who fought them—men like the FBI's Eliot Ness and the "untouchables," whose exploits in the name of law and order became the subject of a popular 1950s television series.

FROM WORLD WAR II TO THE PRESENT

During World War II, the United States used new, awesome weapons of destruction: Sherman tanks, bazookas, grenades, rockets, bombs, and the emerging nuclear arsenals. Two decades later, the nation fought another war in tiny Vietnam. America's air power, rocket power, and firepower achieved a new level of destructiveness and sophistication. Missiles were now electronically controlled and radar guided. The only weapon that didn't change was the .45 Colt automatic.

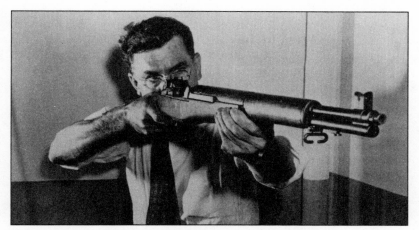

John C. Garand's reliable infantry rifle was the American soldier's "best friend" in World War II. (Courtesy of The Library of Congress)

Chapter 3 reviews gun ownership today. It considers the question of why Americans own guns. It also takes a look at the National Rifle Association and at the attitude of American gunowners toward gun control.

REVIEW QUESTIONS

1. How did the first settlers get their firearms? What were they like?
2. Why is the Kentucky Rifle considered the first distinctly American gun?
3. What kinds of guns were used in the American Revolution? When was each kind of gun most effective?

4. What were some of the changes in gun making between the Revolutionary War and the Civil War?
5. Why weren't breechloaders widely adopted during the Civil War?
6. Explain how gun-toting outlaws have been transformed into heroes.
7. Why were guns important in the Old West?
8. Do you think Americans glamorize violence? Why or why not?

3 Citizens and Guns

There are seventy million gun owners in the United States, according to current estimates. In other words, at least one out of every four Americans owns a gun. But who are these gun owners? How old are they? What is their race and their religion? Where do they live?

Before you continue reading this chapter, consider the statements below. Decide whether each one is true or false. When you are done reading this chapter, see if your ideas about gun owners have changed.

True or False?
- Less than 75 percent of all gun owners are men.
- Most blacks own guns.
- Almost 90 percent of all gun owners are white.
- Most gun owners are single.
- Most gun owners have no more than two guns.
- More gun owners are from the South than from any other region.

WHO OWNS GUNS?

Maybe you have stereotypes from television and newspapers about who owns guns. If so, you may be surprised by the results of a recent *Time Magazine*

CNN poll. If you think that the majority of gun owners are men, you are right. Seventy-five percent of all gun owners are men. Women make up 50 percent of the population. But only 25 percent of all gun owners are women. If you think that most blacks own guns, you are wrong. Black Americans are less likely than white Americans to own guns. Blacks make up 12 percent of the population. But only 6 percent of all gun owners are black. If you think that gun owners are less likely than other Americans to finish college, you are wrong. Just 20 percent of all Americans finish college. But 25 percent of all gun owners do.

Hunters are not all men, as these pheasants discovered. (Idaho, 1920s.) (Courtesy of The Library of Congress)

According to the *Time* poll, the "typical" American gun owner is white, male, under the age of fifty, and southern (most likely) or midwestern. The average number of guns owned was 4.41. Of course, this description of the "typical" American gun owner does not fit *millions* of gun owners. Americans from every race and region own guns—millions of them. And 34 percent of all gun owners are *over* fifty years old.

Earlier polls on gun ownership support the *Time* poll. These polls found that about half of all American men own guns, compared with one-eighth of all American women. They also found that farmers are more likely to own guns than people in other occupations. Protestants are more likely than Catholics, Jews, agnostics, or atheists to be gun owners. So are Republicans compared with Democrats, and the rich compared with the poor.

WHY GUNS?

How many gun owners do you think keep their firearms for protection? Gun violence has been in the news a lot. Many people are afraid. But, in fact, 50 percent of all gun owners polled by *Time* said the main reason they own a gun is for hunting—and this statistic is in keeping with earlier polls. Target shooting accounted for another 9 percent of gun ownership, gun collecting for 5 percent, and 3 percent of gun owners said they keep guns for work. Just 27 percent of gun owners claimed they own a gun for protection. Only 9 percent of those polled had ever fired their gun for protection—compared with 79 percent who had fired for target shooting, 78 percent while hunting, and 43 percent for fun. However, 42 percent of gun owners said that having a gun at home made them feel safer.

THE NATIONAL RIFLE ASSOCIATION (NRA)

Seventy million Americans own guns, and almost three million belong to the NRA. Such numbers give the NRA political clout. With millions of dollars to back it up, the NRA lobby has promoted its philosophy of opposition to gun control. In the 1988 presidential election, the NRA spent 1.5 million dollars to help defeat democratic candidate Michael Dukakis, who favored strong handgun control. Republican George Bush, a life member of the NRA, won their support. He favored stiff penalties for criminals and opposed new federal gun-control measures.

In 1871, after the Civil War, a group of Yankee army officers founded the NRA to promote marksmanship and gun safety. They were embarrassed with the poor training of union soldiers, some of whom could hardly fire their weapons. The NRA was chartered in New York in 1875. In 1908, NRA headquarters moved to Washington, D.C., where it has remained ever since.

The NRA started fighting gun control in the 1930s, when Congress was considering new federal laws to regulate firearms—laws that would require licensing of gun owners and registration of guns. The NRA succeeded in knocking out the licensing and registration provisions from the new legislation.

Through the 1960s, the NRA remained mainly a group of sportsmen and collectors who were dedicated to safety and markmanship. After the passage of the 1968 federal Gun Control Act, however, the organization began an aggressive campaign against gun control. They established the Institute for Legislative Action—a lobbying division that fights gun control by applying political pressure on legislators and legislative candidates. With the support of President Ronald Reagan, the NRA successfully promoted the Firearms Owner's Protection Act of 1986. Through the late 1980s, the organization also helped to defeat state gun-control legislation and to prevent passage of the Brady Bill—a federal law that would require a seven-day waiting period to purchase a handgun (see Chapter 5). Today, the NRA continues to fight gun control and to foster gun safety and marksmanship.

Although known for fighting gun-control laws, the NRA also promotes gun safety and marksmanship. (Copyright Washington Post; *reprinted by permission of the D.C. Public Library)*

GUN OWNERS AND GUN CONTROL

Given the NRA's strong anti-control stand, you might expect that most gun owners oppose gun-control legislation. But the majority of gun owners—according to the *Time* poll—support mandatory registration of semiautomatic weapons (73 percent), handguns and pistols (72 percent). At least half of all gun owners also favor registration of shotguns and rifles. And 87 percent support a seven-day waiting period and a background check for anyone who wishes to buy a handgun. These findings are in keeping with earlier polls.

CRIMINALS AND GUNS

How are criminals different from law-abiding Americans when it comes to guns? Answer the following questions to check your ideas on this subject.

- Do criminals own more guns than the average American gun owner?
- How do criminals get guns? (Do they buy them or steal them?)
- Why do criminals get guns? (Is it for crime or for other purposes?)
- What kinds of guns do criminals prefer?
- When do criminals carry guns?
- Why do criminals fire their guns?

To answer these questions, sociologists James Wright and Peter Rossi surveyed 2,000 convicts—all males incarcerated in state prisons for felony offenses. About 40 percent of their sample said they had never used a weapon to commit a crime. About 50 percent had committed at least one gun crime.

Wright and Rossi found that criminals are more likely to own guns than the general public. They also found that criminals who do own guns have more—6.6 guns on the average—than the "typical," law-abiding American gun owner. Among these felons, handguns were the preferred weapons, followed by sawed-off shotguns. More than 50 percent said they had got their most recent firearm for self-defense—compared with 28 percent who had obtained a gun for a criminal purpose.

About 30 percent of the convicts carried a gun all the time. The most common reason for firing their gun was target shooting and plinking; followed by hunting; both shooting and hunting; self-defense; and, finally, crime. The convicts said that their main reason for using a gun during a crime was for intimidation (69 percent) or self-protection (38 percent). Of those who fired a gun during a crime, slightly over half said they had not planned to do so. In short, criminals, like law-abiding gun owners, acquire and use guns for a variety of purposes. However, the profile of *why* criminals buy guns and *how* they use them is different. For criminals, the emphasis is on self-defense, intimidation, and crime.

Criminals also differed from the general public in the way they obtained their guns. The 1968 Gun Control Act prohibits selling a firearm to a convicted felon. Wright and Rossi found that only 16 percent of the inmates in their study bought their guns through retail outlets. The felons were able to circumvent gun-control laws. Over 70 percent of the convicts purchased or stole their guns from family members or friends.

Wright and Rossi also questioned the convicts

about what they would do if faced with new handgun regulations. The majority of the felons said that they would borrow or steal the handguns if the price were increased. They would buy more expensive handguns if cheap handguns were banned. And they would use sawed-off shotguns or rifles if all handguns were banned.

In the next two chapters, you will be reading about gun control. As you review both sides of the gun-control debate, keep in mind what you have learned about guns and gun ownership. Consider the information you now have about criminals and their guns.

REVIEW QUESTIONS

1. What is the profile of the typical American gun owner?
2. Do you know anyone who does not fit this profile?
3. How many guns does the average gun owner have? How many guns does the average felon have?
4. What is the Institute for Legislative Action?
5. In what way did the NRA begin to change in the 1930s? In the 1960s? Why?
6. Why do criminals get guns? How does this pattern compare with that of the typical gun owner?
7. How do felons get around gun-control laws to obtain guns?
8. Were you surprised by anything you learned about American gun owners? Explain.
9. Were you surprised by anything you learned about criminals and guns? Explain.

4 | What Is Gun Control?

Gun control has different definitions—depending on whom you ask. Imagine the following conversation between some *pro-* gun controllers and *anti-* gun controllers. Like many Americans, they each have different ideas about what gun control means.

Pro– gun control 1: The U.S. Congress should ban the manufacture and sale of all firearms to stop the mad proliferation of guns in America.

Anti– gun control 1: Banning firearms is unconstitutional. The Second Amendment guarantees the right of any American to own firearms.

Pro– gun control 2: Let's keep firearms out of the hands of criminals. Congress should pass a law requiring a seven-day waiting period to get a gun so that authorities can check an applicant's background.

Anti– gun control 2: Criminals will steal guns if they can't buy them. A waiting period will only keep guns out of the hands of law-abiding citizens.

Pro– gun control 3: Cars must be registered. Why not guns? The federal government should require the registration of all guns.

Anti– gun control 3: Registration is the first step toward confiscation of guns. It happened when the Nazis took over Denmark. It could happen here.

Pro– gun control 4: Rifles and shotguns? Fine. They're sports guns. But let's ban handguns. They're only good for one thing—killing human beings.

Anti– gun control 4: Guns don't kill—people do. Impose stiffer penalties on murderers and thieves who use guns to commit crimes. But let law-abiding citizens keep their handguns.

THE SECOND AMENDMENT

The Second Amendment to the Constitution states: "A well-regulated militia being necessary to the security of a free State, the right of the people to keep and bear arms shall not be infringed."

The Second Amendment is one of ten amendments to the U.S. Constitution. Taken together, these amendments are known as the Bill of Rights. The founding fathers—patriots like Thomas Jefferson, James Madison, and Samuel Adams—considered the "right to bear arms" one of the fundamental rights of free people, along with freedom of speech, press, and religion. The Bill of Rights was included in the Constitution to guarantee all Americans these freedoms. But Americans disagree about how to interpret this "right to bear arms."

Pro- Gun Control and the Second Amendment

Pro- gun controllers stress the first part of the amendment: "A *well-regulated militia* being necessary to the security of a free state." They argue that the Second Amendment was intended to guarantee each state the right to maintain armed militia—or national guards under the jurisdiction of each state governor. This was a right that England had tried to deny the American colonies. It was one of the issues that helped trigger the Revolutionary War.

Before the war, England had increased taxes and had stationed English troops throughout the thirteen colonies. The colonists responded by stockpiling arms and organizing militia. When British troops tried to disarm them, fighting broke out. Gun-control advocates claim that the Second Amendment was intended to protect state militia from being disarmed by the federal government, in response to the way England had tried to disarm the colonial militia. So, according to this argument, it does not apply to individual ownership.

Pro- gun controllers also point to four separate Supreme Court decisions:

- *United States v. Cruikshank* (1876)
- *Presser v. Illinois* (1886)
- *Miller v. Texas* (1894)
- *United States v. Miller* (1939)

In all four cases, the Supreme Court of the United States held that firearm-control laws are constitutional. Pro-controllers argue that these decisions by the nation's highest court are proof that their interpretation of the Second Amendment is correct.

Anti- Gun Control and the Second Amendment

Anti- gun controllers emphasize the second half of the amendment: "the right of the people to keep and bear arms shall not be infringed." They have a different interpretation of the Revolutionary War period. They stress the colonists' stockpiling of arms, British prohibitions on gun and ammunition shipments, and British efforts to confiscate weapons at Lexington. This attempt to seize colonial weapons led to the first important Revolutionary War battle. Anti- gun controllers claim that the Second Amendment was meant to protect individuals from being disarmed in the way the British had tried to disarm the colonials. So, according to this argument, it does apply to individual ownership, not just to militia.

To further support their position, anti- gun controllers trace the right to own arms back to pre- Revolutionary war laws—laws which the founding fathers were aware of. The English Bill of Rights (1689), for instance, allowed Protestants to own arms for defense. Also, some early colonial militia laws *required* civilians to own firearms. For example, a Virginia colony law (1623) stated that "men not go to work in the ground [on the land] without their arms and a centinell [sentinel] upon them." Anti- gun controllers cite these laws as proof that the men who wrote the U.S. Constitution meant to protect individual gun ownership.

KINDS OF GUN-CONTROL LAWS

Many cities and states as well as the federal government have enacted gun-control laws. These laws fall into four basic categories.

Where-and-How Laws

The majority of American gun-control laws *regulate where and how* firearms may be used. Where-and-how laws answer these questions:

- Can firearms be concealed, or must they be in plain view?
- Can they be carried in a car?
- Can they be carried upon the person?
- Can they be carried in public places?
- Can they be carried in the street?
- Can they be loaded, or must they be unloaded?

Of course, the answers may be very different— depending on where you live. Portland, Oregon, for instance, prohibits any person from carrying or transporting a loaded firearm on the street or in a public place. In Massachusetts, under the Bartley-Fox Amendment, anyone carrying a handgun without a license—or a long gun without a firearm identification card—is subject to a year in prison. Renton, Washington, prohibits carrying a firearm near a business that sells alcohol by the drink. California requires the registration of all assault weapons. In Washington, D.C., it is unlawful to have a handgun that was not registered as of February 5, 1977.

Licensing, Registration, Waiting Periods

Laws in this category require *licensing, registration, or waiting periods* to purchase a gun. They allow the city, state, or locality to check an applicant's background and/or reasons for owning a gun. Twenty-two states require a permit to carry a handgun openly. Nine states require a permit to purchase a handgun, while six states have a waiting period, four states require an owner's license, and three states require registration.

Most states prohibit people with serious criminal records from owning guns. Other high-risk groups that may be excluded from gun ownership are alcoholics, drug abusers, fugitives, aliens, people with violent histories, and the mentally incompetent—as well as minors.

The states vary dramatically in the way they screen applicants. In most states the burden of proof is on the authorities—to show that an applicant should be excluded from owning a gun. The absence of a waiting period or a short waiting period, however, may mean that authorities cannot conduct a thorough check of an applicant's background. South Dakota, for instance, has a forty-eight-hour waiting period to purchase a handgun. New York and Massachusetts, unlike most states, require applicants to prove good character and good reason for gun ownership.

Bans and Restrictions

Still other laws *restrict or ban certain kinds of guns,* for instance, handguns or semiautomatic rifles. In 1981, Morton Grove, Illinois, a Chicago suburb, passed the first U.S. law prohibiting handgun ownership and sales. The U.S. Supreme Court upheld this law. After that, a number of other cities—such as San Francisco, California; Cincinnati, Ohio; and Chicago, Wilmette, Highland Park, Deerfield, and Winnetka, Illinois— instituted similar laws. In 1988, the state of Maryland outlawed the sale and manufacture of cheap handguns ("Saturday night specials").

Sometimes violent incidents lead to legislation. In

1989, Patrick Purdy, a mentally disturbed drifter, mowed down a group of Stockton, California, elementary school children with a semiautomatic assault rifle. There was a public outcry. Soon after, the federal government banned the importing of semiautomatic weapons. A number of cities—such as Stockton, California; Los Angeles, California; and Cleveland, Ohio—also outlawed their manufacture or sale. A number of state legislatures are considering similar laws.

Stiff Sentencing

Other gun-control laws impose *stiff sentences on people convicted of gun crimes.* Anti- gun controllers tend to support these laws. They believe that mandatory sentences for gun crimes will act as a deterrent to crime in general and gun crime in particular. Public Law 99-308 (May 1986)—a federal law—requires an extra five years' imprisonment in federal cases for first offenders and an extra ten years' imprisonment in federal cases for repeat offenders who use a gun to carry out a violent crime or a drug-trafficking crime.

What has the federal government done about gun control? What are the gun-control laws in your state? Chapter 5 explains the history of gun control and will help you understand the laws that affect you.

REVIEW QUESTIONS

1. How do pro- gun controllers interpret the Second Amendment?

2. How do anti- gun controllers interpret the Second Amendment?
3. What are the four basic categories of gun laws? Which is the most common type?
4. Why do violent incidents sometimes lead to gun-control legislation?
5. Why do anti- gun controllers favor stiff sentences for people convicted of gun crimes?
6. What category of gun laws do you support? Why?

5 More About Gun Control

You may be surprised by some of the information in this chapter. For example:

- The United States has 20,000 gun laws on record today.
- The first American gun-control laws existed before the Revolutionary War.
- Gangsters helped bring about the first federal gun-control laws.
- One American city requires all heads of households to own a firearm.

How did the United States get 20,000 gun laws? Who makes these laws? What are the anti- gun controllers doing about it? What is happening with gun control today?

STATE AND LOCAL GUN LAWS

The first American gun-control laws were written before the Revolutionary War—before there was a federal government. The Massachusetts Bay Colony, for instance, had a law that prohibited colonists from carrying guns in public places.

After the American Revolution, some states passed gun-control legislation. In 1804, New Jersey outlawed dueling after Aaron Burr shot Alexander Hamilton (both were famous political figures of that period). In 1813, Kentucky passed a law that made it illegal to carry concealed weapons, and, soon after that, so did Georgia, Indiana, Louisiana, Alabama, and Arkansas. During the period from 1880 to 1915, other states and localities followed suit. Today many states have restrictions on carrying concealed weapons.

An Uneven Patchwork

The patchwork of American gun laws is uneven. Some states, like Massachusetts, have very strict gun laws. In Massachusetts, a person can go to jail for carrying a handgun without a license. Other states, like New Hampshire, where many residents are hunters, have much more lenient gun laws. Most state gun laws concern handguns rather than long guns (see Chapter 4). Hawaii is the only state that requires registration of long guns; New Jersey, Massachusetts, and Illinois require both a permit to purchase a long gun and an owner's license. You can check the Appendix at the back of this book to find out about the gun laws in your state.

Keep in mind that the gun regulations where you live may differ significantly from your state laws. New York City, for instance, has many more restrictions on gun ownership than does New York State. And Kennesaw, Georgia, has an ordinance (1982) that requires all heads of households to own guns and ammunition. Kennesaw passed this law around the time that Morton Grove, Illinois, banned firearms. The Kennesaw law reaffirmed the citizen's right to own firearms.

Preemption Laws

Many cities and localities have passed gun-control laws that are stricter than their state laws. To counter this trend, the National Rifle Association (NRA) promotes *preemption laws*. These laws prohibit cities and localities from enacting their own restrictive gun-control legislation—outside the jurisdiction of the state. Many police groups are opposed to preemption laws because they remove gun legislation from local control. Philadelphia, Pennsylvania, tried to pass a law requiring applicants to submit a "permit-to-purchase-handguns" form for police approval. The U.S. Supreme Court held the Philadelphia law unconstitutional because a Pennsylvania preemption law makes gun control a state matter. The city council in Atlanta, Georgia, also failed to institute strict gun controls because of Georgia's preemption law. Today thirty-eight states have preemption laws. Check the Appendix at the back of the book to find the legislative status of your state.

FEDERAL GUN LAWS

Over the years, the federal government's attitude toward gun control has tended to be "hands-off." Most of the 20,000 gun laws on record are state and local laws. One reason is a strong reluctance by the federal government to infringe on Second Amendment rights. Another is the powerful gun lobby, headed by the NRA. And from 1880 to 1915 substantial gun-control legislation appeared at the state and local levels—yet another reason the federal government was slow to legislate controls on firearms. The first federal gun-control laws—in the early 1900s—were aimed at explosives rather than guns *per se*.

The Roaring Twenties

Then came Prohibition and the Roaring Twenties. As gangsters battled to control the illegal liquor trade, Americans started worrying about the rise in crime. By 1924, congressmen had filed more than a dozen federal gun bills. In 1927, Congress made it illegal to mail concealable firearms to private citizens. But this attempt to stop the mail-order trade of guns was undermined by a loophole in the law. Firearms could still be *ordered* through the U.S. mail and *delivered* by other carriers.

The Tough Thirties

In the 1930s, Americans were getting nervous about machine-gun-toting gangsters like John Dillinger Under President Franklin Delano Roosevelt, Congress passed the National Firearms Act of 1934 and the Federal Firearms Act of 1938. The 1934 law made it more difficult for citizens to keep gangster-style weapons such as machine guns, submachine guns, sawed-off shotguns, and silencers. The 1938 law was the first to regulate the manufacture, possession, and sale of many kinds of firearms.

The Rock-Throwing Sixties

During the next thirty years, the only federal firearms legislation was the Federal Aviation Act of 1958. This law made it illegal to carry firearms on passenger flights.

But the 1960s were a time of upheaval. President

John F. Kennedy was assassinated in Dallas, Texas, on November 22, 1963. A few years later, rioting rocked the inner cities. Strikes and protests against the Vietnam War shook many college campuses. Then gunfire struck down two more public figures: Martin Luther King in Memphis on April 4, 1968, and Robert Kennedy in Los Angeles on June 5, 1968. New federal gun-control legislation was enacted in the aftermath of this violence and the public outcry that followed.

The Gun Control Act of 1968

The Gun Control Act of 1968 included the following provisions:

1. It required federal licensing and inspection of fire-arm dealers under new, stricter guidelines.
2. It restricted the sale of firearms and ammunition between states.
3. It outlawed the importation of "Saturday night special" handguns.
4. It prohibited high-risk groups from owning fire-arms.
5. It established additional penalties for using fire-arms to commit a federal crime.
6. It forbid private citizens from owning "destructive devices" such as machine guns, bazookas, bombs, or grenades.

VICTORIES FOR OPPONENTS OF GUN CONTROL

Despite being badly wounded by a "Saturday night special," Ronald Reagan, a life member of the NRA, supported anti- gun-control measures throughout his presidency. In 1986, the McClure-Volkmer Bill passed Congress. This bill, also known as the Firearms Owner's Protection Act, was a major victory for anti- gun controllers. It loosened or repealed several provisions of the 1968 Gun Control Act. For example, the 1968 ban on interstate sale of rifles and shotguns was repealed. Standards for federal licensing and inspection of dealers were also loosened. However, the McClure-Volkmer *increased* the penalties for carrying or using firearms during a violent federal crime—in keeping with the position of anti-controllers who favor stiffer penalties for felons who commit gun crimes.

GUN CONTROL TODAY

In recent years, Congress has been debating another gun-control bill—the Handgun Violence Prevention Act, also known as the Brady Bill. It calls for a waiting period of seven days to screen applicants who wish to purchase a handgun. The Brady Amendment is named after Sarah Brady and James Brady, who was Ronald Reagan's press secretary. James Brady was shot and seriously wounded during the assassination attempt on the president. The Bradys have been fighting for gun control since then. In March 1991, Reagan gave a strongly worded surprise endorsement of the Brady Bill—reversing his opposition to new Federal gun controls—and on May 8, the House of Representatives passed the bill.

One of the basic issues within the gun-control debate is gun violence. Chapter 6 looks at the complex problem of gun violence and asks you to consider

-- James S. Brady --
President Reagan's Press Secretary
Shot on March 30, 1981 by John Hinckley

This handgun statistic just broke his silence

"Add your voice to mine. Help me beat the gun lobby.

Ever since I was shot, I have watched from my wheelchair as the gun lobby blocked one sane handgun control proposal after another.

But I'm not just watching anymore. I'm calling on Congress to pass a common sense law -- the Brady Bill -- requiring a seven-day "cooling-off" period before the purchase of a handgun so police have time to check if the buyer has a criminal record.

The Brady Bill (S.1236 & H.R.467) will save thousands of lives and prevent tens of thousands of crippling injuries. 91% of the American people -- *and 87% of American handgun owners* -- support it. And so does every major law enforcement organization in the country.

In fact, it seems the only people against the Brady Bill are psychopaths, criminals, drug dealers and the gun lobby.

So why hasn't Congress passed it? Because too many members of Congress are afraid of the gun lobby and too many take the gun lobby's PAC money.

In the last six years -- while handguns were killing 120,000 Americans -- the gun lobby poured $4 million into Congress' pockets to block sane handgun laws.

The gun lobbyists say a seven-day wait is "inconvenient." I'd like to see one of them try spending a day in my wheelchair.

Can we beat the gun lobby? YES -- if we raise our voices together, we can send Congress a message they can't ignore: vote this bill in or we'll vote you out."

Here's all I'm asking you to do and it's real easy.

Just call 1-900-226-4455

and for only $2.75, charged to your phone bill, we'll send a letter in your name to your Representative supporting the Brady Bill. We'll also send you a copy.

Help me break the gun lobby's stranglehold on Congress!

This public safety message brought to you by Handgun Control, Inc. 1225 Eye St., NW, Washington, DC 20005

Both sides in the gun-control fight use the media to gain support. This pro- gun-control advertisement, endorsing the Brady Bill, was produced by Handgun Control, Inc.

two important questions: What causes gun violence? What can we do about it?

REVIEW QUESTIONS

1. Why are most of the 20,000 gun laws either state or local laws?
2. Look back to Chapter 4, pages 42–45, at the four categories of gun laws. Which category do the following laws fall into: the Massachusetts Bay Colony law that prohibited colonists from carrying guns in public places; the National Firearms Act of 1934; the Brady Bill?
3. How did a loophole undermine the 1968 Gun Control Act?
4. Why do you think important federal gun-control bills were enacted in the 1920s, 1930s, and 1960s?
5. What kind of problems might occur when one state has stricter gun-control laws than its neighbor?
6. Explain why the McClure-Volkmer Bill was a victory for anti-control groups.

6 Guns and Violence: The Other Arms Race

- An angry husband, separated from his pregnant wife, kidnaps her in a car and shoots her to death.
- A mentally ill babysitter enters an elementary school with a pistol. She murders one student and wounds five others.
- A teenager, depressed about his low grades, takes out his father's gun and kills himself.
- A ten-year-old, at home alone with his little sister, pulls a gun from his parents' nightstand and shoots her by accident.
- An unemployed ex-convict holds up a liquor store at gunpoint, wounding three employees.
- A neo-Nazi terrorist, furious at a liberal radio-talk-show host, guns down the celebrity outside his car.

The names, the faces, and the circumstances change, but the message remains the same: Gun violence is a part of modern American life. Television and newspapers catalog the daily rash of gun homocides, gun suicides, gun terrorism, and gun crime.

Can Americans do anything to stop gun violence? For some, the answer is more laws. For others, it's more guns.

THE STATISTICS

The United States is the most violent nation in the Western world. The U.S. murder rate is almost three times higher than Canada's and over seven times higher than Great Britain's. In 1985, five Canadians died by handguns; eight British died by handguns; forty-six Japanese died by handguns; and 8,092 Americans died by handguns. Over 30,000 Americans died by *firearms* the following year.

Many of the statistics in this section refer to the overall murder rate—not just to gun murders. But keep in mind that in the United States three out of five murders are committed with a gun. One American is murdered with a gun every forty minutes— and for each person killed by gunfire, *five* others are *wounded*. Every two years, guns kill more Americans than did the whole Vietnam War.

No geographical region, race, or gender is immune to violence in America. However, certain groups and regions suffer a higher rate of violence than others. For example, in 1989, the southern states accounted for 42.9 percent of all murders, with a murder rate of eleven per 100,000 population. By comparison, midwestern states accounted for 18.6 percent of all murders, with a murder rate of seven per 100,000. Also, about 75 percent of all murder victims were males— most of them murdered by other males. Likewise, nine out of ten *female* murder victims were killed by a male. Over 63 percent of all homicide victims were under the age of thirty-four. Significantly, 50 percent of all murder victims in 1989 were black, but blacks accounted for just 12 percent of the population. Among young, inner-city black men, homicide is the leading cause of death.

Relatively few homicides are interracial. In 1989, 94 percent of black murder victims were killed by blacks; similarly, 86 percent of white murder victims were slain by whites. Over 50 percent of all murder victims were killed by people they knew.

Despite these gruesome figures, the U.S. murder rate has declined by 3.5 percent since the record year of 1980, when there were 23,040 murders. In 1989, the murder rate was nine per 100,000—compared with 10.2 percent in 1980. Many experts believe that one reason for this decline is the aging of the U.S. population as the post-World War II "baby boom" generation grows up. In other words, older people are less likely to kill. They also point to improved medical emergency treatment that has helped keep gunshot victims alive.

Unfortunately, the number of murders has increased slightly in recent years—from 20,100 (in 1987) to 20,680 (in 1988) to 21,500 (in 1989). Most criminologists agree that mild fluctuations in the murder rate from year to year do not represent a trend. Some experts, however, worry that deadlier street weapons and increased drug traffic may continue to push up the murder rate. But others say that drug-related murders have always been prevalent.

SUICIDES

During the 1980s, the U.S. suicide rate increased. So did the number of suicides among people under the age of twenty-four and the number of suicides committed with guns. In 1986, 64 percent of male suicides and 40 percent of female suicides ended their lives with a gun. Yet psychologists believe that many people who attempt suicide do not really want to die. They estimate that for every suicide, there are twenty attempted suicides. These *attempted* suicides suggest that many people who try to take their own lives may really want to be rescued. But those who attempt to kill themselves with guns succeed at the rate of 94 percent. As one doctor put it, "guns are a permanent solution to a temporary problem."

ONE WEEK IN MAY

The statistics give you only the hard facts—not the names or faces of the victims or the pain and suffering of their families. One week in May 1989, however, *Time* magazine opted in favor of faces over statistics. They kept a tally of all the Americans who died from gunshot wounds during that week.

As the authors of the article put it, "events like these happen so often that Americans' sense of horror and outrage has been numbed. Death by gunfire has become nearly as banal in the United States as auto fatalities: shootings are so routine that they are sometimes ignored by the local news. Only by coming face-to-face with the needless victims does the wastefulness sink in."

The article cataloged 464 deaths. The story ran for over thirty pages. The profile of victims represented a cross-section of America. They ranged in age from two to eighty-seven. They were white, black, Asian, and Hispanic. They came from forty-two different states. Many were poor, young, sick, abandoned, or old. They died from accidents, homicides, and suicides. Most of the murder victims knew their assailants. Suicide was the most common cause of death—accounting for 216, or almost half, of the victims.

AN EMOTIONAL ISSUE: MORE LAWS?

On the morning of January 17, 1989, Patrick Purdy—an angry, twenty-six-year-old drifter—entered a playground at the Grover Cleveland Elementary School in Stockton, California. The playground was filled with children and several teachers. He sprayed about 100 bullets from his AK-47 semiautomatic rifle into the crowd. Five children died; and twenty-nine children and one teacher were wounded—before Purdy killed himself with a 9 mm pistol. Said one eyewitness on an ABC news special a week later: "I wake up during the night sometimes and I think about them. I see one or two of those little bodies lying there, the pink tennis shoes, the mittens and the gloves, the scarves, the school books. It's ingrained in me forever. I drive by schoolyards that are right near the freeway on the way to work every day and I still cringe, looking at children in the yard, thinking, 'They're not even safe there.' "

The story of the Stockton playground killings ran on the evening news. Across the country, there was an outcry. Many Americans, like the eyewitness quoted above, were wondering why children aren't safe in a playground.

For pro- gun controllers, the answer was simple: "Get rid of the guns." And, in fact, the Stockton massacre, like several other violent incidents of the past, did lead to new laws. In the weeks that followed, the California legislature outlawed the manufacture and sale of semiautomatic weapons. In two dozen other states, legislatures considered similar laws. President Bush banned the importing of five types of semiautomatic weapons. And Colt Industries stopped the sale of AR-15 semiautomatic rifles.

AN EMOTIONAL ISSUE: MORE GUNS?

To the question "Why aren't children safe in a playground," anti- gun controllers have another answer—and different stories to tell.

The following two reports appeared in the February 1990 and the December 1989 issues of the *American Rifleman:*

In December 1989, two teenagers from Manchester, Connecticut, jumped a sixty-eight-year-old woman in a parking lot. They knocked her to the ground and tried to steal her purse. When the woman refused to let go of it, the boys began dragging her across the lot. At that point, Mark Sheehan, a parcel-service driver, witnessed the assault and came to the woman's aid.

One of the assailants pulled a wrench on Sheehan, who then took out his gun and shot the teen. After the police arrived, they charged the boys with first-degree robbery, larceny, and assault on a person over sixty years old. (First reported in the *Courant,* Hartford, Connecticut, December 9, 1989.)

Early one morning in September 1989, a nineteen-year-old woman answered the door of her Champaign, Illinois, home. A strange man asked to use her phone. The woman agreed. The man pretended to make a call, but when the woman insisted that he leave, the man pushed her into her bedroom. There, the woman pulled a handgun from the holster she kept on her headboard. She forced her assailant out of the house and called the police. (First reported in the *News-Gazette*, Champaign, Illinois, September 20, 1989.)

For anti- gun controllers, stories such as these—which appear regularly in the *American Rifleman*—illustrate the value of keeping a gun for protection.

WHY SO MUCH VIOLENCE?

This is a question much in dispute.

Those who favor gun control believe that guns—and the American attitude toward guns—foster violence. By passing stronger gun-control laws, they say, criminals will get fewer guns; in the process, *the attitude that guns can solve problems* will change. As a result, there will be less violence on American streets and in American homes—or so the argument goes.

Those who oppose gun control argue that the court system gives violent offenders the message that crime is risk-free because only a small percentage of felons go to jail. Automatic jail sentences for gun crimes will help keep violent criminals off the streets and cut down on such violence—or so the argument goes.

But many experts and court officials suggest that deep social problems—not guns or lenient jail sentencing—foster violence. They point to the chain of poverty, poor nutrition, and despair; to the lure of easy drug money—money that could help pay for food and rent; to inadequate schools, which produce graduates who cannot read; to single-parent or broken families with overburdened mothers and uninvolved fathers.

Others argue that exposure to television and movie violence contributes to violence in American society. The media, they say, romanticize violence, guns, and even criminals—in movies such as *Lethal Weapon, The Untouchables, Die Hard, RoboCop,* and *48 Hrs.*—and teach children aggressive behaviors.

The subject of gun violence has led to yet another hot question: Who is responsible for the damage caused by a gun? The person who handles the gun? The gun owner? Or the gun manufacturer? And what if the "offender" is a young child? Chapter 7 considers the issue of gun responsibility to help you decide how to answer these questions.

REVIEW QUESTIONS

1. How do the number of American gun deaths compare with the number of American deaths caused by the Vietnam War?
2. How is suicide a "permanent solution to a temporary problem"?
3. What two answers have people found to the question "How do we stop gun violence?" Which answer do you support? Explain why.
4. What groups are most likely to become victims of gun violence?
5. What effect did the Stockton massacre have on gun control? Why do you think this was so?

6. What are some of the theories about the causes of gun violence? What answers to this question do pro- gun controllers and anti- gun controllers offer? What do you think?
7. Why do some people call gun violence an epidemic?
8. Did any of the statistics on gun violence surprise you? Explain.

7 | Gun Responsibility

Who is responsible when a child gets hold of a gun? The child? The gun owner? The manufacturer?

THE CASE OF OMAR SOTO

In 1988, Omar Soto, a ten-year-old Florida boy, was watching the movie *Gotcha* with a friend. The movie included scenes where college students played a game called "gotcha" with fake guns. Omar's friend ran home for some real guns to show his friend. He pulled out three loaded firearms that belonged to his father. One was a .357 magnum. When he tried to uncock the gun, it fired, shooting Omar in the head and killing him.

No charges were filed, because no one was *legally* responsible—not according to Florida law. When Judy Soto, Omar's mother, asked law officers what they could do in a case like Omar's, they answered, "File and close it."

Judy Soto's response was, "No way you are closing my son's case." For eighteen months, Omar's parents campaigned to make adults legally responsible for loaded guns in their homes. At first they were not successful. Then, in June 1989, three Florida children died and two were seriously wounded in gun accidents. Gunfire replaced motor vehicle accidents as the leading cause of death among children. By the fall of 1989, following a public outcry, the Florida legislature passed a law holding parents responsible for gun injuries caused by their children.

The new law did not apply to the case of Omar Soto, however, because it was passed after his death. But the Sotos convinced the state to file manslaughter charges against the boy who had killed their son. He was convicted and sentenced to 100 hours of community service teaching other children about the dangers of playing with guns.

PRODUCT LIABILITY

When fifteen-year-old Ken Hacker shot and paralyzed a schoolmate in 1977, a Dallas law firm sued the companies that manufactured and sold the gun Hacker used.

In the 1985 case of *Kelly v. R. G. Industries,* a Maryland man filed suit against the company that manufactured the Roehm revolver used to shoot him in the chest during a robbery.

After James J. Robertson committed suicide with a handgun, his family filed a wrongful death lawsuit in 1986 against Grogan Investments—the company that sold him the handgun.

In the case of *Bernethy v. Walt Failor's Inc.,* another wrongful death suit was brought against a retail store that was responsible for supplying an intoxicated man with a rifle. In 1978, the man had used the rifle to shoot and kill his wife in the tavern where they had been drinking.

To date, no product liability suit against a gun manufacturer or retailer has been successful. But some anti-controllers worry—and some pro-controllers hope—that eventually a gun manufacturer or retailer will be held responsible for the misuse of their products.

ACCIDENTS

Many Americans listening to television news the first week in June 1989 heard a chilling 911 emergency broadcast. Sean Smith and his sister Erin had been playing with their father's handgun. Sean did not know that it was loaded. He fired the gun and shot his eight-year-old sister in the head. Sean's anguished cries brought home the terrible reality of what can happen when children play with loaded guns.

A California study of accidental gun deaths by children found:

- Most of the accidents occurred in a residence.
- Typically, when the accident occurred, the children were playing with a gun that had been stored loaded but out of sight.
- 40 percent of the deaths were self-inflicted.
- The shooter was a family member in 24 percent of the cases and a playmate in 35 percent of the cases.
- The shooter was a boy between the ages of ten and fourteen in 70 percent of the cases.
- Handguns were involved in almost 60 percent of the cases.

The number of gun accidents decreased by almost 25 percent between 1978 and 1988—from 1,806 firearm accidents in 1978 to 1,400 in 1988. This decline in gun-accident fatalities is in keeping with the downward trend in gun accidents over this century. Some experts attribute this decline to organized hunter training programs. (Hunting accidents account for about 40 percent of gun accidents, according to some estimates.) However, in 1988, there was an 8 percent increase in gun accidents over the year before. Every day a child is killed by an accident at home.

GUN SAFETY

As you might imagine, everyone does *not* agree on the best route to gun safety. For instance, some experts recommend that guns in the house should always be kept unloaded—with the firearm on one floor and the ammunition on another. Others insist that a locked drawer is sufficient protection against accidents. Still others argue for "child-proofing" firearms with special locks to keep them secure against children, just as pill bottles are now child-proofed. But some gun owners worry that too many precautions can make their firearms useless for immediate protection. And some gun controllers say that having *no gun* is the only certain way to ensure gun safety.

Many people on both sides of the gun debate believe that education can help prevent many gun accidents. Some school courses teach children about the danger of guns. These courses get children to think about the best way to deal with situations involving firearms. They teach young students that it is not safe to be around guns without adult supervision and parental permission. They also counsel

Which is more dangerous, the pistol or the crime it's supposed to prevent? (*Copyright* Washington Post; *reprinted by permission of the D.C. Public Library*)

young people never to touch a gun, to leave the area if they see one, and to call an adult for help.

For over 100 years, the NRA has offered training courses for hunters and gun owners. Today, NRA gun-safety programs are in over 500 schools and school systems. Thousands of NRA members volunteer as certified instructors, hunter safety educators, police firearms trainers, shooting coaches, and training counselors. The NRA also has safety programs for families that do not own guns.

GUN-SAFETY RULES

The following rules are based on NRA gun-safety publications and on the Sporting Arms and Ammunition Manufacturer's Institute "Ten Commandments of Safety."

General Rules for Handling Guns

1. Treat every gun as if it were loaded.
2. Keep the muzzle pointed in a safe direction.
3. Never put your finger on the trigger—until ready to shoot. Keep the safety on.
4. Keep the gun *unloaded*—until ready to use. Store your gun and ammunition separately.

General Rules for Shooting Guns

5. Learn how your gun operates.
6. Never point a gun at anything you don't want to shoot.
7. Make sure of your target. Don't shoot at hard or flat surfaces or at water.
8. Don't climb fences or trees or jump over a ditch with a loaded gun.

9. Make sure you carry the correct ammunition—and only the correct ammunition—for your gun.
10. Stay away from alcohol or drugs when shooting.

As you can see, you can do something about gun safety. Keep these rules in mind, and treat guns with respect and caution.

REVIEW QUESTIONS

1. How did the case of Omar Soto change Florida law?
2. In what kinds of cases have manufacturers been sued for the misuse of their products? What was the outcome?
3. What has been the trend in the number of gun accidents in the last decade? Why do you think this is so?
4. What basic guidelines do gun-safety programs teach children?
5. What are some general rules for handling guns? For shooting them?
6. Who do you think should be held responsible when a child gets hold of a gun? Why?
7. How do you think gun owners should ensure safety at home?
8. What would you do if you knew that a friend of yours had his parent's gun? What would you do if you found a firearm outside?

8 | The Future of Guns in America

I f you could look out a window to the future of guns in America, what would you see?

- Fewer guns?
- Less gun violence?
- New gun-control laws?
- More gun-safety programs?

One way to keep a clear view from the window is to separate the issues. The gun debate has many parts: gun ownership, gun violence, gun responsibility, criminals and guns, gun control, and gun education. When these issues get mixed up, the view gets foggy. Treating the different parts separately helps clear the air.

WILL AMERICANS MANUFACTURE AND OWN MORE GUNS?

American gun ownership has been fairly consistent through the 1980s, with almost 50 percent of all American households having a gun. That rate is unlikely to *decrease* significantly through the 1990s unless Congress changes the rules for purchasing a specific class of firearms, such as handguns.

Likewise, an *increase* in the rate of gun ownership over the next decade appears doubtful for several reasons. Some cities and states have banned assault weapons or handguns or tightened gun regulations in recent years. Furthermore, the rate of gun ownership has declined slightly since the mid-1970s.

Also, American gun manufacturing has declined about 25 percent since the early 1980s. In 1989, gun manufacturers produced 4.09 million guns, down from 5.16 million in 1982. The experts suggest several reasons for this decline. One reason is lower defense budgets—with the military buying fewer guns. New gun-control legislation may also deter some gun manufacturers. Finally, there is the saturated gun market; many people who want guns already have them. Given these factors, the experts say, this decline will continue as a trend through the 1990s.

If fewer guns are manufactured through the 1990s, there might be a modest decline in gun ownership. Why modest? Guns have a long life span—twenty-five to seventy-five years. Given the estimated 200 million guns currently in circulation, the effect of reduced gun manufacturing on ownership probably would not be significant.

WILL THERE BE MORE GUN CONTROL?

Slowly but surely, there will be more gun control during the next decade—or so say many experts. As always, most gun-control battles will be fought on the state and local level. And, as always, most of the battles for licensing, permits, background checks, and waiting periods will be lost. But not all of them.

In the 1980s, several cities and states passed legislation aimed at handguns and assault weapons. More will do so in the 1990s. In some cases, violent episodes like the massacre in Stockton, California, will lead to legislative victories for gun control.

On a small scale, some cities and states may try unusual approaches to gun control. The city of Baltimore, Maryland, sponsored a gun buyback in the 1980s when Baltimore citizens turned over to the police 17,000 guns in return for payment. Boston, Massachusetts, is planning a similar drive in the 1990s to get Bostonians to turn over their guns. A few communities may enact measures that reflect the research on criminal use and ownership of guns. For example, legislation could require enhanced security measures such as child-proofing or safes for gun-owning homes and businesses; special insurance provisions for gun owners; stiff penalties for gun theft; and documentation of theft or sale of guns.

On the federal level, efforts to pass the Brady Bill were given a big boost when former president Ronald Reagan, a longtime opponent of gun-control legislation, gave his strong endorsement of the measure. The House of Representatives passed the bill in May 1991. The future of the Brady Bill, however, depends upon two important issues: Will it pass the Senate? And, if so, will President Bush veto it?

On the other hand, the NRA will continue to press for legislation that favors firearm owners: preemption laws, hunter-protection legislation, and reform of concealed-weapon laws. Considering the NRA's record during the 1980s, it is likely to have continued success with this program.

More often, the two sides will also reach compromises—as they did in Oregon in 1990. The Oregon legislature enacted a fifteen-day waiting period and background check for handguns and long guns. In return, the NRA received some lessening of Oregon's concealed-weapons statute. This movement toward compromise may be the most important trend of the 1990s. In fact, some experts believe that the Brady Bill could become law *along with* a strong anti-crime package favored by those who oppose gun control.

CAN AMERICANS DO ANYTHING ABOUT GUN VIOLENCE?

Gun violence is an emotional issue. Both sides in the gun debate have offered proposals that some advocates claim will reduce gun violence. Through the 1990s, some gun-control advocates will continue to promote licensing, registration, and longer waiting periods in the name of crime prevention. Likewise, some anti-gun-control advocates will push for stricter sentences to punish criminals—especially those who use guns in crime.

But will these measures reduce gun crime? On this question, there is little agreement among the experts. The Wright and Rossi study of felons and their guns (Chapter 3) shows that criminals, in general, do not get their guns from retail outlets. But many gun-control regulations—registration, licensing, and waiting periods—are directed toward retail gun customers. So these laws may not have much effect on gun crime. The study also shows that criminals acquire guns for protection. So the prospect of a felon's associates or victims having guns, as Wright and Rossi point out, may be more threatening than the prospect of an extra year in prison. In other words, stricter sentences for gun crime may not work either.

On the other hand, gun violence has declined since the early 1980s. As you might imagine, the reasons for this decline are also in dispute. Some experts say that it is the natural result of the "aging of America"—given that young people are most prone to gun violence. The aging factor will continue to figure in the issue of gun violence through the 1990s, according to this point of view. But others argue that slight *increases* in gun violence in the late 1980s suggest a more ominous trend. Drug disputes, deadlier weapons, and more young people involved in gun crime would mean a continued increase in gun homicides and violent crime, according to this point of view.

WILL THE NRA LOSE ITS FIREPOWER?

The NRA will continue to be a potent voice against gun control. However, some critics believe that the organization will lose some firepower in the 1990s. They point to the growing strength of gun-control groups, to a recent decline in NRA membership, to the dozens of new state and local gun-control proposals, and to the loss of support by police organizations that occurred when the NRA backed the sale of armor-piercing bullets and plastic handguns, both of which threaten the lives of police officers.

On the other hand, NRA spokesmen say that their critics' prognosis is wishful thinking. They point to a high success rate in defeating gun-control legislation in the 1980s and to the passage of preemption laws and hunters'-rights statutes in many states. They also say that their polls of on-line officers show that the rank-and-file police officers still support the NRA. As far as their membership is concerned, the NRA claims that the decline occurred as a result of an increase in membership dues. The situation, they say, has already turned around.

HOW WILL GUN-EDUCATION PROGRAMS FARE?

Neither side in the gun debate disputes the importance of gun-education programs. Many states—including Florida, West Virginia, Virginia, and Oklahoma—already have gun-safety programs in their schools. Others are likely to follow.

SUMMING IT UP

In general, the view from the window to the future of guns in America won't change dramatically in the 1990s. Americans will still buy guns. Pro- gun controllers will push for more gun laws. Anti- gun controllers will try to stop them and, in most cases, will succeed. In the meantime, more teachers will inform their students about gun safety and help them understand the gun debate.

REVIEW QUESTIONS

1. How has the rate of gun ownership changed since the early 1970s?
2. What are some reasons the experts give for the decline in gun manufacturing?
3. Why do some critics think the NRA may lose some of its firepower in the 1990s?
4. Why do supporters of the NRA say their critics are just thinking wishfully?
5. Do you think gun violence will decline in the 1990s? Why?
6. Do you think there will be more gun control in the 1990s? Why?

CONCLUSION

On both sides of the gun debate, many Americans have taken a strong stand. What about you? Do you worry that Americans could lose their freedom to own firearms? Do you believe that more gun control is needed? Or do you think that compromise is the best solution?

Now that you have read about the different parts of the gun debate, you can support your position with facts and statistics. On the other hand, you recognize that each side interprets this information in its own way—and that some of this information is in dispute.

What else can you do? Educating yourself and others about guns in America is important. Whatever your point of view, you can learn more about gun-control legislation in your state. You can discuss your ideas with your friends. At school, you can lobby to get gun-safety courses or write an editorial for the school newspaper, stating your ideas on gun control.

You can take an active stand in the gun-control debate. You can get involved on the state level by writing your legislators or on the national level by encouraging your congressmen to vote for your position. You can find out where your legislators stand on the issue, and you can help elect officials who take your side in the gun debate. Finally, you can lend your support to pro- gun control or anti- gun control groups, such as Gun Control, Inc. and the National Rifle Association (NRA). (See addresses in the Appendix.)

When it comes to gun accidents, you can also make a difference. You know that guns are dangerous in the hands of children or in the hands of untrained adults. Before you turn eighteen, you can make sure that you never touch a gun—or a part of a gun— without adult supervision. You can call an adult or you can call 911 if you see anyone with a gun who is under the age of eighteen. You can discourage your friends from touching or carrying guns.

You know that "gun abuse," like drug and alcohol abuse, often leads to tragedy. So you can refuse to participate in any games that involve guns—loaded or unloaded. You can call 911 if you know of anyone who is handling a gun under the influence of drugs or alcohol.

Gun violence is a giant problem—like drugs and poverty. It won't go away overnight. But you can help. If you don't like the present picture of *Guns in America*, it's up to you to change it.

APPENDIX

COMPENDIUM OF STATE LAWS GOVERNING HANDGUNS
1990

Compiled by the NRA Institute for Legislative Action

The following chart lists the main provisions of state handgun laws as of May 1990. In addition to the state provisions, the purchase, sale and, in certain circumstances, the possession and interstate transportation of firearms is regulated by the Federal Gun Control Act of 1968 as amended by the Firearms Owners' Protection Act. Also, cities and localities may have their own handgun ordinances in addition to federal and state restrictions. Details may be obtained by contacting local law enforcement authorities or by consulting your state's firearms law digest compiled by the NRA Institute for Legislative Action.

SINCE STATE LAWS ARE SUBJECT TO FREQUENT CHANGE, THIS CHART IS NOT TO BE CONSIDERED AS LEGAL ADVICE OR A RESTATEMENT OF THE LAW.

NOTE: State constitutional provisions on firearms vary considerably. The Connecticut constitution serves as an example of the basic features contained in the constitutions of many states: "Every citizen has a right to bear arms in defense of himself and the state." (Article 1, Section 15)

STATE	PURCHASE				CARRYING				OWNERSHIP	
	Application and Waiting Period	License or Permit to Purchase	Registration	Record of Sales Sent State or Local Govt.	Carrying Openly Prohibited	Carrying Concealed Prohibited	License to Carry Openly	License to Carry Concealed	Owner Licensing or I.D. Cards	Constitutional Provision
ALABAMA	X			X		X	X[1]	X		X
ALASKA						X				X
ARIZONA					X[2]	X[2]				X
ARKANSAS						X				X
CALIFORNIA	X			X		X		X		
COLORADO	X							X		X
CONNECTICUT	X			X		X	X	X		X
DELAWARE								X		X
FLORIDA	X[10]						X	X		X
GEORGIA							X	X		X
HAWAII	X	X	X	X		X	X	X		X

HANDGUNS

ILLINOIS
INDIANA
IOWA
KANSAS
KENTUCKY
LOUISIANA
MAINE
MARYLAND
MASSACHUSETTS
MICHIGAN
MINNESOTA
MISSISSIPPI
MISSOURI
MONTANA
NEBRASKA
NEVADA
NEW HAMPSHIRE
NEW JERSEY
NEW MEXICO
NEW YORK
NORTH CAROLINA
NORTH DAKOTA
OHIO
OKLAHOMA
OREGON
PENNSYLVANIA
RHODE ISLAND
SOUTH CAROLINA
SOUTH DAKOTA
TENNESSEE
TEXAS
UTAH
VERMONT
VIRGINIA
WASHINGTON
WEST VIRGINIA
WISCONSIN
WYOMING
DISTRICT OF COLUMBIA

[1] License to carry in a vehicle either openly or concealed.

[2] Arkansas prohibits carrying "with a purpose to employ it as a weapon against a person." Tennessee prohibits carrying "with the intent to go armed."

[3] Chicago only.

[4] Loaded.

[5] Handguns must be presented to the city chief of police or county sheriff to obtain a certificate of inspection.

[6] Permission to carry concealed may be granted by county sheriff on written application.

[7] Handguns prohibited in Evanston, Oak Park, Morton Grove, Winnetka, Wilmette, and Highland Park.

[8] Some municipalities control the possession, sale, transfer or carrying of handguns; e.g. Cleveland and Columbus require a police permit for purchase; Toledo requires a handgun owners' I.D.; Cincinnati requires application for purchase. In addition, some forbid the possession and sale of handguns with a certain magazine capacity, usually 20 rounds or more.

[9] Prohibits carrying a firearm "with the intent or purpose of injuring another."

[10] Certain cities or counties.

[11] Applies only to pre-registered firearms. No new handguns can be brought into the city.

NL3N0659

R.9/90 10M

RESOURCES

The following organizations are involved in firearms and gun-control issues. Virtually all of them have an interest in one side or another of the gun-control debate. Contact them for more information.

Center to Prevent Handgun Violence
1125 I Street NW, Suite 1100
Washington D.C. 20005
(202) 289–7319

Works to educate the American public about the risks and responsibilities of owning a handgun. Sponsors programs for junior and senior high school students that include reviews of interpretations of constitutional guarantees to firearm ownership, discussions of the role of the handgun in society, and causes and methods of preventing handgun violence. Conducts research and compiles statistics. Affiliated with Handgun Control, Inc. (see below).

**Citizens Committee for the Right
to Keep and Bear Arms**
Liberty Park
12500 N.E. Tenth Place
Bellevue, WA 98005
(206) 454–4011

Describes itself as composed of citizens interested in defending the Second Amendment, with more than 150 members of Congress serving on its advisory board. Conducts educational and political activities, weekend seminars, and in-depth studies on gun legislation. Sponsors a speakers' bureau and compiles statistics.

Educational Fund to End Handgun Violence
110 Maryland Avenue NE
Washington D.C. 20002
(202) 544–7227

Deals with public educational matters concerning handgun violence, particularly as it affects children. Provides assistance to litigants, victims, attorneys, and legal scholars. Helps develop materials and educational programs for schools in an effort to convince teenagers not to carry guns. Works to ban the sale of high-powered BB guns. Examines impact of handguns on public health. Also concerned with automatic-weapons violence. Conducts research, maintains speakers' bureau, compiles statistics. Affiliated with National Coalition to Ban Handguns (see below).

Gun Owners of America
8001 Forbes Place, Suite 102
Springfield VA 22151
(703) 321–8585

Preserves and defends the rights of gun owners at the local, state, and federal levels through lobbying efforts and political action. Conducts seminars to inform the public, the media, and government officials about key issues affecting the Second Amendment. Publishes books and articles, and sells videocassettes, concerning gun issues and how they affect people throughout the world. Opposes bans on semiautomatic weapons, armor-piercing bullets, and handguns.

Gun Owners Incorporated
5457 Diablo Drive, Suite 1
Sacramento CA 95842
(916) 349–1812

An organization of persons contributing funds to the defense of Americans' right to "safely and legally" own firearms. Advocates harsher punishment for criminals misusing firearms. Keeps members informed on legislation concerning gun control. Compiles statistics, bestows awards; conducts lobbying and political research.

Handgun Control, Inc.
1225 I Street N.W., Suite 1100
Washington D.C. 20005
(202) 898–0792

Public citizens' lobby working for legislative controls and governmental regulations on the manufacture, importation, sale, transfer, and civilian possession of handguns. Compiles up-to-date information on the handgun issue, including statistics, legislation, and research. Maintains speakers' bureau; bestows awards. Publishes books, newsletter, and pamphlets.

National Board for the Promotion of Rifle Practice
Pulaski Building, Room 1205
20 Massachusetts Avenue, NW
Washington D.C. 20314
(202) 272–0810

An agency of the Office of the Secretary of the Army, as directed by Title 10, United States Code, to promote marksmanship training outside the active services of the Armed Forces. Offers civilian shooting clubs and marksmanship clubs in high schools and colleges. Provides arms and ammunition to member clubs; exhibits national marksmanship trophies; maintains records and distributes awards for national and international marksmanship competitions.

National Coalition to Ban Handguns
100 Maryland Avenue N.E.
Washington D.C. 20002
(202) 544–7190

National educational, professional, and religious organizations united to seek a ban on the private sale and possession of handguns in America. (Exceptions to the ban would include the police, active military personnel, federally licensed collectors, and target shooters whose handguns are used and kept only at shooting clubs.) Works to enact restrictive handgun controls at local, state, and national levels; assists state and local handgun control organizations. Conducts research and compiles statistics in a number of areas including handgun suicide, homicide, and accidents; handgun production and sale; and lobbying efforts of pro-handgun organizations. Conducts political action and educational activities, and maintains speakers' bureau.

National Rifle Association of America
1600 Rhode Island Avenue N.W.
Washington D.C. 20036
(202) 828–6000

An organization of target shooters, hunters, gun collectors, gunsmiths, police officers, and others interested in firearms. Promotes rifle, pistol, and shotgun shooting, hunting, gun collecting, home firearm safety, and wildlife conservation. Encourages civilian marksmanship. Educates police firearms instructors. Maintains national and international records of shooting competitions; sponsors teams to compete in world championships. Also maintains comprehensive collections of antique and modern firearms. Administers the NRA Political Victory Fund. Bestows awards; compiles statistics; sponsors research and education programs; maintains speakers' bureau and museum, lobbies on firearms issues. Publishes magazines and pamphlets.

National Shooting Sports Foundation
555 Danbury Road
Wilton CT 06897
(203) 762-1320

Supported by manufacturers of firearms and ammunition, accessories, components, gun sights, hunting clothes, and other reputable firms that make a profit from hunting and shooting, including publishers of outdoor and gun magazines. Strives to foster a better understanding and more active participation in the shooting sports. Promotes firearms safety; works with state and federal agencies in providing additional hunting opportunities; cooperates with private enterprise to create outdoor recreational facilities. Distributes literature on firearms safety, conservation, and recreational shooting. Finances educational programs. Publishes newsletter and annual directory.

ISSUES AND QUESTIONS OF GUN CONTROL

The following is excerpted from a report by Harry Hogan of the Congressional Research Service. It is concerned with the role government may play in issues of gun control, especially concerning the misuse of guns and "assault weapons."

Supporters of more restrictive Federal controls on firearms contend that such controls are needed to curb access to these weapons by criminals, juveniles, and other "high risk" individuals. They argue that the violent crime rate (and also the fatal accident rate) has a positive relationship to the availability of guns, and that, in general, only Federal measures can succeed in reducing this availability. Opposition to Federal controls (existing and proposed) varies widely in nature and degree and may be based on constitutional positions, the belief that gun controls are not in fact a crime deterrent, the belief that widespread gun ownership does deter crime as well as potential government tyranny, or a combination of these.

Positions

The January 1989 killing of five children in a Stockton, California, schoolyard, and the wounding of nearly thirty others, again revived the national debate on gun control. In the sense that it concerns a federal role, this debate began in the 1920s. Its early phase resulted in the enactment of two Federal statutes designed to reduce the availability of guns to criminals and to disclose to the Government the ownership of especially lethal guns. These laws, passed in the 1930s, remained for the most part unchallenged until the early 1960s, when a Senate committee investigating juvenile delinquency turned its attention to the effects of a flourishing mail-order trade in firearms. This inquiry led to a major revision of the existing statutes in 1968.

The Gun Control Act of 1968 is considered too moderate by some and too restrictive by others, and both camps have regularly pressed for amendments. Until 1986, only minor changes were approved; in that year, Congress passed the "McClure-Volkmer amendments" making a number of modifications sought by the National Rifle Association and other groups and individuals concerned with what they saw as oppressive provisions of the law and of its implementation. As passed, however, the same amendments included several provisions to strengthen restrictions.

Since 1986, principal gun control concerns of Congress have related to: (1) requiring a police check on purchasers of handguns, during a specified waiting period (the "Brady amendment," approved by the House Judiciary Committee in 1988 for inclusion in the omnibus drug bill of that year but failed to pass House); (2) banning production and distribution of armor-piercing ammunition; (3) adding controls on firearms not detectable by devices commonly used at airports and other restricted facilities; and (4) increasing penalties for violent crimes and drug offenses involving firearms, required by the Justice Department feasibility study of developing a system accessible to gun dealers that would facilitate the identification of felons attempting to purchase firearms, and revocating probation for possession of a firearm by a Federal probationer.

The schoolyard tragedy in Stockton, perpetrated by an apparently deranged individual with a lengthy record of criminal arrests and convictions (who subsequently killed himself), resurrected calls for stronger controls. Whereas previous gun regulation efforts had been aimed at handguns, the new drive focussed on the type of gun used in the Stockton incident, a semiautomatic version of the Soviet military assault rifle, the AK-47, and certain semiautomatic shotguns and pistols.

All proposals to restrict the availability of firearms to the public at large raise the same general questions. Is gun control crime control? Would the stricter regulation of firearm commerce or ownership lower the Nation's rates of homicide, robbery, and assault? Would they stop the attacks on public figures or thwart deranged persons and terrorists?

Although firearm suicides and accidents are also advanced as reasons for stronger controls, gun regulation advocates offer as their principal concern the large number of violent crimes committed in this country each year. Pointing to the generally lower crime rates of other industrial nations, these advocates contend that a strict curb on gun ownership and use is a major factor in the difference.

In recent years, proponents of controls have usually held that only a Federal law will be effective in the United States. Otherwise, they say, States with few restrictions will continue to feed black markets in the restrictive States. They believe the Second Amendment to the Constitution, which states that "A well-regulated militia, being necessary to the security of a free state, the right of the people to keep and bear arms shall not be infringed," is: (1) obsolete;

(2) intended solely to guard against suppression of State militias by the central Government and therefore restricted in scope by that intent; or (3) does not in any case guarantee a right that is absolute, but one that can be limited by reasonable requirements. They ask why a private citizen needs any firearm that is not designed primarily for hunting or other recognized sporting purposes.

Opponents of gun control vary in their position with respect to specific forms of control but in general take the view that interdiction laws do not accomplish what is intended. It is just as difficult to keep weapons from being acquired by "high risk" individuals, they argue, as it was to stop the sale and use of liquor during Prohibition. In their view, a regulatory system designed to do this only creates problems for law-abiding citizens and possibly threatens their civil rights. Moreover, they reject the contention that the low crime rates of such countries as England and Japan have anything to do with gun controls, maintaining that multiple cultural differences are responsible instead.

Gun control opponents also reject the assumption that the only legitimate purpose of ownership by a private citizen is recreational (i.e., hunting and target-shooting). They insist on the continuing need of people for effective weapons to defend person and property. They observe that the law enforcement and criminal justice system in the United States has not demonstrated the ability to furnish an adequate measure of public safety. They further uphold the right to keep arms as a defense against potential government tyranny, pointing to numerous examples in other countries of the use of firearm restrictions to curb dissent and consolidate government power.

To supporters of restrictive controls, the opposition is out of touch with the times, dogmatic about the Second Amendment, or lacking in sensitivity or concern for the problems of crime and violence. To opponents, control advocates are naive in their faith in the power of regulation to solve social problems, or moved by emotionally generated hostility to firearms and gun enthusiasts rather than true concern over crime.

A number of commentators have noted that the contemporary battle over gun control in the United States appears in many ways to be a cultural confrontation of "cosmopolitan" and "bedrock" America.

Semiautomatic "Assault Weapons"

General Background. The Federal gun control issue of greatest current interest is whether special restrictions should be imposed on the commerce in, and ownership of, certain military-style semiautomatic firearms: rifles such as Germany's H and K91 and variants of the Soviet Army's AK47; shotguns such as the "Street Sweeper"; and pistols such as the Israeli UZI 9mm and the INTRATEC TEC 9.

Proponents of greater restrictions regard such firearms, which are designated "assault weapons" or "semiautomatic assault weapons," as potentially more lethal than other firearms, and characterize them as "the weapons of choice of drug dealers, violent criminals, terrorists, and psychopaths." Although some also make the point that these guns can be converted to fully automatic (continuing fire as long as the trigger is kept pulled) this does not appear to be essential to the argument as developed by most proponents; the California schoolyard tragedy that precipitated the debate involved a firearm firing in the semiautomatic mode.

Opponents argue that the firearms specifically cited by the opposition, although mostly based on selective fire weapons (capable of fully automatic fire as well as semiautomatic) of military origin, are functionally indistinguishable from semiautomatic generally, many of which are widely used for target shooting and hunting, and for self-defense. Moreover, they maintain that even if a satisfactory distinction could be made, added restrictions would not prevent the guns from being acquired by high-risk individuals, and would merely add to the growing body of controls that constrain only those who abide by the law.

Although the Stockton incident has served as the immediate catalyst for current efforts aimed at semiautomatics, other occurrences in recent years have also generated concern over "Rambo" firearms that many feel are: (1) capable of greater firepower than other, more familiar firearm models; and (2) inherently attractive to certain kinds of criminals or disturbed individuals.

The Bureau of Alcohol, Tobacco, and Firearms (ATF) reports substantial increases in recent years in the importation of such guns as the Chinese-made semiautomatic variants of the AK47, selling in the United States at bargain prices. According to ATF, 8,131 AK47-type guns were imported in the two years ending 1986; during a 14-month period ending Nov. 30, 1988, the total was 40,379.

Under existing Federal law, no firearm or firearm accessory subject to the provisions of the National Firearms Act (i.e., fully automatic firearms, sawed-off long guns, silencers, etc.) may be imported, nor may any surplus military firearm. Otherwise, ATF is required to permit the importation of any gun that is "generally recognized as particularly suitable for or readily adaptable to sporting purposes." From the enactment of the provision in 1968 until 1989, only two long guns were determined to fail this sporting purposes test.

On July 7, 1989, ATF announced a ban on importation of 43 semiautomatic rifle models and "similar types" on grounds that a review has shown they fail to meet the sporting purposes criterion.

Use in Crime. Much of the evidence offered to support the contention that military-style semiautomatic firearms are being increasingly used in the commission of crime is anecdotal. In recent testimony before the Senate Subcommittee on the Constitution, Smithsonian firearms expert Dr. Edward C. Ezell said, "When I have queried forensic specialists working with major law enforcement agencies for information about 'assault rifles' in crimes, I have been told that such data does not exist. Generally it is the 'gut feeling' of police forensics officials that .38 caliber revolvers and 12 gauge shotguns continue to be the primary firearms used in crime and shootings." Perhaps the only systematic effort to gather evidence, thus far, is a survey of State law enforcement agencies conducted in late 1988 by the California Assembly Office of Research. The findings as reported by the Office are as follows:

1. A survey response agency in virtually every county in the State reported the existence of assault weapons (including short-barreled shotguns and rifles).
2. About 83% of the reporting agencies reported either a significant (63%) or moderate (20%) increase in both the number and frequency of use of assault weapons over the past 5 years.
3. Factors associated with the increasing popularity of assault weapons were firepower (rate of fire, magazine capacity, and type of ammunition), status (macho image, exotic appearance), concealability, and the ease with which a person may obtain such weapons.
4. Over 65% of respondents felt that assault weapons are either displacing pistols and revolvers as the weapons of choice or augmenting the firearm arsenal of gang members and criminal offenders.

Additionally, a recent study of ATF firearm traces found that 10% of those conducted in 1988 involved "assault guns." An ATF trace is made at the request of a law enforcement official (Federal, State, or local) and involves a firearm known or suspected to have been used in the commission of a crime.

On the other hand, the Federal Bureau of Investigation (FBI) *Uniform Crime Reports* for 1988 show that the use of any type of rifle in homicide during that year was in the range of 4% and of any type of shotgun in the range of 6% (handgun, 45%; cutting or stabbing, 20.5%). A University of Texas criminologist estimates that homicides committed with military-style semiautomatic long guns constitute less than 1% of the total.

Firepower. So-called firepower depends on a combination of factors, including; (1) velocity of the fired round; (2) size (caliber and amount of powder) of the round; (3) shape and material of the round; (4) rate of fire; (5) sustainability of fire (magazine capacity or ease of replacement of magazine); and (6) effective range. Factors (1), (2), (3), and (6) are principally functions of the ammunition itself (the gun must, of course, be capable of using the ammunition), while (4) and (5) relate almost exclusively to the type of firearm used.

As for the rate of fire, under laboratory conditions a true assault rifle such as the AK47 in full automatic mode can theoretically fire 600 to 750 rounds per minute. In semiautomatic mode, it can be fired as fast as the user can pull the trigger; by one estimate, 60 rounds per minute would be average.

The effective ranges of military assault rifles are 300 to 500 yards, depending upon the ammunition used. The effective ranges of other rifles vary from 150 to 1,000 yards, again depending upon the ammunition. The effective range of a typical handgun is about 50 yards.

Attraction for "High-Risk" Individuals. Another reason given for seeking special controls on the firearms in question is that they have a strong appeal for criminals and disturbed individuals because of their "macho image" or "exotic appearance." In congressional hearings on the subject, a number of witnesses have made this point. Again, although the factor was reported by the California law enforcement survey mentioned above as being "associated with the increasing popularity of assault weapons," the evidence is chiefly anecdotal or conjectural.

Issues

Among the principal questions posed by the gun-control issue are:

1. Is availability of guns and/or ammunition a major or substantial factor in the violent crime rate? In the incidence of fatal or crippling accidents? Or, on the contrary, is widespread gun ownership a crime deterrent, as some studies have suggested?
2. Can availability of firearms to the "high-risk" individuals who misuse them be curbed by legal controls?
3. If added controls are desirable, what form should they take?
4. Should such controls be Federal or State?
5. Would certain proposed controls violate the Bill of Rights guaranty of the right to keep and bear arms?
6. If Federal, would they infringe on the police powers that some authorities hold are reserved to the States under the Tenth Amendment?
7. Would the benefits of controls outweigh the burdens or discontent they might cause?
8. Assuming a broad reading of the Second Amendment, is there nevertheless a limit on the *kinds* of arms whose ownership and use should be protected? If so, where should the line be drawn? At firearms or devices that cannot be considered "personal weapons"? If so, at firearms capable of fully automatic fire (or capable of being easily converted to such)? At any gun without a recog-

nized sporting purpose (not recognizing a right to a gun designed purely for self-defense)? At any concealable gun? At any gun based on a military prototype?

9. Do guns provide an effective mode of defense of self and property, or does their presence—as the authors of at least one study have claimed—increase a risk to the owner, his family, and friends?

10. As a criminogenic factor in contemporary America, is gun availability on the same level as factors relating to general operation of the criminal justice system (lack of police manpower, crowded court calendars, plea bargaining and other legal maneuvering by defendants, use of probation or truncated sentences in some jurisdictions because of overpopulated prisons, etc.)?

11. Practically, can controls be achieved (e.g., would it be possible to gain public acquiescence to a law prohibiting private ownership of handguns generally or semiautomatic long guns and pistols that have become widely used)? Would effective enforcement be possible?

Specific proposals raise the following questions:

1. Does the Gun Control Act's basic concept of regulation through Federal licensing of persons involved in gun and ammunition commerce provide a satisfactory framework for solving the gun-crime problem, or must there be some system of direct Government restrictions on the individual gun owner (such as universal registration or licensing for ownership, as in the case of the

machine guns, sawed-off long guns, and destructive devices)?

2. To keep guns (handguns or otherwise) out of the hands of criminals and irresponsible persons, is it necessary to reduce general gun availability through selective bans or licensing requirements, or would the restrictions provided by a police background check (during a specified waiting period or on-the-spot) be sufficient? (Would either approach accomplish the objective?)

3. If the goal is reduction of gun availability, how far must a reduction policy be taken and how is the reduction best handled? Can handgun prohibitions be limited to a class of handguns that causes the greatest trouble (assuming such a class can be identified), or will it be necessary to include all handguns in the prohibition? In view of the current concern over semiautomatic "assault weapons," could the same questions be asked with respect to rifles and shotguns?

4. Are there any legitimate needs for the military-style semiautomatic rifles, shotguns, and pistols that are the object of pending Federal legislation as well as of a number of State legislative proposals?

5. Do available data on the use of semiautomatic "assault weapons" support the position that such guns are being used by criminals to an extent that justifies stronger controls?

6. Can so-called semiautomatic "assault weapons" be satisfactorily distinguished, for legislative and administrative purposes, from semiautomatic firearms widely used for hunting and target-shooting purposes, as well as for self-defense?

7. Are semiautomatic "assault weapons" more lethal—i.e., capable of greater firepower (velocity plus range plus rate of fire) than other semiautomatic firearms? Or is their popularity with some criminals and mentally deranged individuals owing simply to their military and "Rambo" associations?
8. If the principal objection to semiautomatic "assault weapons" is that they are capable of accepting large-capacity magazines (perhaps defined as holding more than 10 rounds of ammunition)—thus making it possible to fire a large number of rounds without pausing to change magazines—would a ban exclusively aimed at such magazines, rather than the guns that will accept them, have the desired effect?
9. Should any firearm or firearm accessory ban be directed at further manufacture and transfer, or should it "reach into the home" and affect actual gun (or accessory) ownership when the prohibition becomes effective?
10. If new controls were to succeed in making it hard for criminals to acquire other concealable firearms (or semiautomatic "assault weapons"), would they revert to the sawed-off long guns of the 1920s and 1930s?

OPPOSING POINTS OF VIEW

The following are statements of purpose from just two of the many organizations involved on both sides of the gun control debate (see *Resources*, above). They are taken from mailings the organizations use to get new members.

From Gun Owners of America

Americans have an individual right to keep and bear arms. The constitutional protection of this right was reaffirmed in 1990 by a strong majority of the Supreme Court (*U.S. v. Verdugo-Urquidez*).

The founders wanted this protection in the Constitution to insure that the government would never have a monopoly of force. Madison, the author of the second amendment "right of the people to keep and bear arms," pointed out that the other governments of the world were despotisms because they did not trust their people with firearms.

After the Civil War, blacks were being disarmed and killed by the Ku Klux Klan in the South. One of the main reasons the fourteenth amendment was enacted was to require the states to respect the second amendment protections their citizens were afforded in the Bill of Rights.

Today, Americans use firearms over 2,700 times a day to ward off criminal attack. They do this very responsibly, because three quarters of them find it necessary to simply brandish their weapon without firing it. Yet when they do fire, armed citizens kill, in justifiable homicide, twice as many criminals as police do. This is understandable when one considers that there are only 150,000 police on duty at any one time to protect 250,000,000 Americans.

The second amendment is like fire insurance. Hopefully it never has to be used. But if the people are ever faced with tyranny, or if a person is ever faced with imminent harm by a criminal, getting a gun after the fact will do no more good than getting insurance after the house has burned down.

From the Center to Prevent Handgun Violence

More than 25 million households own some 60 million handguns; half these weapons are kept loaded. The results are tragic—loaded, easily accessible handguns in the home are a major cause of injury and death in America. They are the leading weapon used in accidental shootings among children, in suicides, and in domestic homicides. More than 22,000 Americans are killed each year by handguns. Many of these tragedies could be prevented if handgun owners and those considering a purchase understood the risks and responsibilities of handgun ownership.

The Center to Prevent Handgun Violence is a national, education, legal action and research organization established in 1983 by Pete Shields to reduce handgun deaths and injuries. The Center's goal is to research, pioneer, and evaluate programs—with the guidance and assistance of influential intermediaries from the education, health, legal, law enforcement and entertainment communities—which promote an understanding of the dangers and responsibilities of handgun ownership.

Current Center efforts include: 1) our "Gun-Violence-Free Generation," consisting of the nation's first school gun violence prevention curriculum, now in five school districts. The curriculum is currently being worked into a national model. Additionally, with the American Academy of Pediatrics, child safety materials are being prepared for parents to be distributed by pediatricians; 2) public service announcements for television and radio; 3) public education campaigns on handgun safety conducted with law enforcement; 4) our Legal Action Project, which provides legal counsel for handgun violence victims and states/municipalities defending gun laws; 5) innovative film and television programming, and connections with the entertainment community; and 6) unique research on the scope of handgun violence.

The Center's expertise in the problems of handgun violence and alliances with other organizations and individuals involved with violence makes us the logical choice to assist schools and communities in their efforts to stem this epidemic of handgun violence in our country.

GLOSSARY

Ammunition. The shells or cartridges fired from a gun.

Anti- gun control. Favoring no restrictions on the access of law-abiding citizens to firearm ownership.

Armor-piercing bullets. A type of bullet that can penetrate protective vests or other gear sometimes worn by law-enforcement officers.

Assailant. A person who attacks, kills, or wounds another person.

Background check. A type of gun control requiring review of the background of a potential gun owner to check for a criminal record or history of drug or alcohol abuse.

Ban. A law or act that prohibits the acquisition or sale of a particular item, such as gun.

Child-proofing. Making potentially dangerous products safer for children by adding special locks, attachments, or other features.

Concealable weapons. A weapon, such as a handgun or sawed-off shotgun, that can be easily hidden or concealed.

Concealed-carry law. A gun-control law that restricts citizens from carrying concealed weapons on their person and/or in a vehicle.

Controversial. Tending to stir up conflict, disagreement, and controversy; a controversial issue.

Duel. A formal combat between two adversaries that generally involves witnesses; a gun duel.

Felon. A person who commits a serious or violent crime.

Felony. A serious or violent crime, as distinguished from a misdemeanor, that generally results in a jail sentence upon conviction.

Firearm. A device for storing, firing, and aiming ammunition.

Gun. A firearm.

Gun buy-back. A policy that permits city, state, or local authorities to pay residents in exchange for their guns.

Gun-control law. Any law that restricts the ownership or sale of firearms.

Gun licensing. A type of gun control requiring gun owners to have licenses or permits for keeping guns in their homes and/or carrying them in public.

Gun registration. A type of gun-control requiring gun owners to register or record their ownership with government authorities.

Handgun. A short, thick-barreled firearm that can be hand-held.

Homicide. Murder.

Hunter-protection legislation. Laws that protect the rights of hunters.

Interracial. Between different races of people. Murder victims are generally of the same race as their assailants; interracial murders are much rarer.

Lobby. An organization that uses its political power to promote causes supported by its membership.

Magazine. A device for holding extra cartridges in a firearm.

Murder rate. The number of murders per year per 100,000 people in a given locality or country.

Muzzle. The mouth or opening of a firearm.

National Rifle Association. An anti- gun-control

lobbying organization that supports the rights of gun owners while also promoting marksmanship and gun safety.

Plastic handgun. A type of lightweight handgun made mostly of plastic. Many proponents of handgun control favor banning or restricting the use of plastic handguns, because they are allegedly more difficult to detect in gun-detection systems.

Poll. A record of public opinion based on random questioning of people in a given location.

Preemption law. A law that prohibits cities and localities from enacting restrictive gun-control legislation outside state jurisdiction; preemption laws are favored by anti– gun-control advocates.

Pro- gun control. Favoring restrictions on the access of citizens to firearm ownership.

Product liability. Accountability by a manufacturer or retailer for damages brought about by the use or misuse of their product.

Rifle: A long, thick-barreled firearm with a handle that fits to the shoulder.

Saturday night special. A small, cheap, poorly made handgun that is easy to purchase on the street.

Sawed-off shotgun. A shotgun in which the barrel has been sawed off for concealment.

Second Amendment. One of ten amendments to the U.S. Constitution. The Second Amendment protects the right of American citizens to bear arms. Americans disagree about how to interpret this amendment.

Semiautomatic. A firearm with a removable magazine and a trigger that must be pulled once to fire each shot.

Shotgun. A long, thin-barreled firearm.

Statistics. Numerical information or data scientifically collected and analyzed.

Suicide. A self-inflicted death.

Victim. A person who suffers as the result of the actions of another person.

Waiting period. A type of gun control that gives a city, state, or locality sufficient time to check an applicant's background before issuing a gun permit.

BIBLIOGRAPHY

BOOKS

Akehurst, Richard. *Antique Weapons, for Pleasure and Investment*. New York, Arco Publishing, 1969.

Bakal, Carl. *The Right to Bear Arms*. New York, McGraw-Hill, 1966.

Cline, Victor, ed. *Where Do You Draw the Line?* Provo, Utah, Brigham Young University Press, 1974.

Dolan, Edward F. *Gun Control: A Decision for Americans*. New York, Franklin Watts, 1982.

Forbis, William, and the editors of Time-Life Books. *The Cowboys*. New York, Time-Life Books, 1973.

Gallup, George, Jr. *The Gallup Poll: Public Opinion 1988*. Wilmington, Del., Scholarly Resources, 1989.

Gottlieb, Alan. *The Gun Grabbers*. Bellevue, Wash., Merrill Press, 1986.

———. *Gun Rights Fact Book*. Bellevue, Wash., Merrill Press, 1988.

Hardy, David T. *Origins and Development of the Second Amendment*. Southport, Conn., Blacksmith, 1986.

Long, Robert Emmet, ed. *Gun Control: The Reference Shelf, v. 60, n.6*. Bronx, N.Y., H. W. Wilson, 1989.

Niemi, Richard G.; Mueller, John; Smith, Tom W. *Trends in Public Opinion: A Compendium of Survey Data*. New York, Greenwood Press, 1989.

Peterson, Harold. *Pageant of the Gun*. Garden City, N.Y., Doubleday, 1967.

Sherrill, Robert. *The Saturday Night Special*. New York, Charterhouse, 1973.

Shields, Pete. *Guns Don't Die—People Do*. New York, Arbor House, 1981.

Siegel, Mark A.; Jacob, Nancy A.; Foster, Carol R. *Gun Control.* Wylie, Tex.: Information Plus, 1989.

Tunis, Edwin. *Weapons, a Pictorial History.* New York, World Publishing/Times Mirror, 1954.

Warner, Ken, ed. *Gun Digest 1987/41st Annual Edition.* Illinois, DBI Books, 1986.

Wright, James D., and Rossi, Peter H. *Armed and Considered Dangerous.* New York, Aldine de Gryter, 1986.

Zimring, Franklin E., and Hawkins, Gordon. *The Citizen's Guide to Gun Control.* New York, Macmillan, 1987.

NEWSPAPER AND MAGAZINE ARTICLES

"The Armed Citizen." *American Rifleman,* December 1989 and February 1990.

"Gunning for Assault Rifles." *Time Magazine,* March 27, 1989.

Hinds, Michael deCourcy. "Number of Killings Soars in Big Cities Across United States." *New York Times,* July 18, 1990.

Kaye, Steven. "Top Guns." *The Washingtonian,* June 1989.

Lenzi, John C. "The Second Amendment—a Decade in Review." *American Rifleman,* March 1990.

McNamara, Joseph D. "A Nation of Certified Killers." *Harpers Magazine,* May 1989.

Maranz, Matthew. "Guns 'R' Us." *The New Republic,* January 23, 1989.

Matchan, Linda. "City's Woes Resound in Dorchester Court." *Boston Globe,* May 27, 1990.

"The NRA Shoots Itself in the Foot." *Business Week,* May 16, 1988.

"The Other Arms Race." *Time Magazine,* February 6, 1989.

Rikhoff, Jim. "Mixed Bag." *American Rifleman,* January 1989.

"Seven Deadly Days." *Time Magazine,* July 17, 1989.

"Tiny Fingers on the Trigger." *U.S. News & World Report,* July 3, 1989.

Tye, Larry, "NRA Loses Firepower." *Boston Globe,* June 11, 1990.

"Under Fire." *Time Magazine,* January 29, 1990.

Wintemute, Garen, M.D.; Teret, Stephen; Kraus, Jess; Wright, Mona; Bradfield, Gretchen. "When Children Shoot Children: 88 Unintended Deaths in California." *Journal of the American Medical Association (JAMA),* June 12, 1987.

Zent, John. "A Tradition of Safety." *American Rifleman,* April 1990.

Special Reports, Pamphlets, Television News Specials, and Transcripts

"ABC News Special: Guns in America." News report and ABC/"Time" Forum, January 24, 1990.

"Children and Guns." "Prime Time," March 1990.

Federal Bureau of Investigation. *Uniform Crime Reports for the United States.* Washington, D.C., 1989.

National Rifle Association. "At Home with Guns." Washington, D.C.

———. "Gun Safety: Instructional Guidelines." Washington, D.C.

———. "NRA Home Firearms Responsibility." Washington, D.C., 1962. (student manual)

———. "A Parent's Guide to Gun Safety." Washington, D.C., 1988.

National Safety Council. *Accident Facts.* Chicago, 1989.

NRA Institute for Legislative Action. "Your State Firearms Laws." Washington, D.C., June 1989.

U.S. Treasury Department, Bureau of Alcohol, Tobacco and Firearms. *Annual Firearms Manufacturing and Exportation Report.* Washington, D.C., October 1981–December 1989.

———. *State Laws and Published Ordinances.* Washington, D.C., 1988.

INDEX